WHY IS THERE ALWAYS ANGELS AROUND US?

ANGELS
AROUND US

"*The angel of the Lord encamps around those*
Who fear Him, and He delivers them."
Psalm 34:7

MISS NONNE

ISBN 978-1-64559-197-9 (Paperback)
ISBN 978-1-64559-198-6 (Digital)

Covenant Books, Inc.
11661 Hwy 707
Murrells Inlet, SC 29576
www.covenantbooks.com

Presented:

By:

Date:

"For He will command his angels concerning you to guard you in all your ways." Psalms 91:11

Angel of Hope painted for me by Susan in 2004

This book is dedicated to my sweet husband, Ronald (deceased), to our children, Sherri Lynn (deceased); Julie Ann and her husband, Drew; and Ronald and his wife, Kristi. Also, all my precious grandchildren, Brikken, Merlyn, Saffron, Edison, Jaclyn, Mitchell, and Jared (deceased). To my brother, Larry, and his wife, Charlotte. I love you all more! Nonne! To all of you dear ones that have encouraged me to seek truth and lived life with me, thank you!

Before Grandchildren
Ronnie, Kristi, Julie, Drew, Phyllis, Ron

My family (2009)
Back row: Brikken, Julie, Drew, Merlyn, Nonne
Front row: Edison, Mitchell, Jaclyn, Saffron, Ron, Jared, Kristi

CONTENTS

About the Book

God has always been with me in a real way. As a very young girl on a farm in Iowa, I learned about God and His angels from my Aunt Olive. I can remember playing dolls with someone, yet there were not any little girls living near us. I believe my guardian angel was at my side even before my birth, protecting me. The older I became, the more aware I was of God's guarding, protecting, and providing of angels in my life. The veil for me between the natural/physical and the supernatural/spiritual is getting thinner. God's angels are ready to help us at all times. We just need to ask God to send them in our time of need. Many things that happen in our lives we call a coincidence. Is it possible that many things that happen are God's incidence? "Do not neglect to show hospitality to strangers, for by this some have entertained angels without knowing it." (Hebrews 13:2)

O Lord you alone are my hope.
I've trusted you, O Lord from childhood.
Yes, you have been with me from birth;
from my mother's womb you have cared for me.
No wonder I am always praising you!
My life is an example to many,
because you have been my strength and protection.
That is why I never stop praising you;
I declare your glory all day long. (Psalm 71:5–8)

Dick's 43rd birthday in hospital
Birth of Sonshine the Clown

INTRODUCTION

"For I know the plans I have for you, plans to prosper you and not to harm you, plans to give you hope and a future." (Jeremiah 29:11) In 1970, I had never read this promise of God. If I had, I would not have believed it would have been meant for me. Our firstborn, Sherri Lynn, died that year; she was nine years old.

I became very angry with God. I had many questions I wanted answered. I began a search for the meaning of life and death. I desperately needed to find peace. This search for peace in my life brought me full circle back to God in 1975. Oh, what a joy I have today remembering that sweet grace and peace of Jesus as He welcomed me back into His loving arms. I knew I needed to learn more about the Giver of this peace and joy that I was experiencing. I started attending Bible studies and gathered for prayer with other believers. I was searching for God's plan for my life. Within the year, I became deeply committed to the Lord and His work. I truly believed that God's promises were for my life. I began to trust God with more and more of my life.

In May 1981, my father died suddenly of a heart attack. Two weeks later, our dear friend Dick was facing a possible amputation of his arm. In just a few days, Dick would be forty-three years old. No one felt much like celebrating. My husband, Ron, and I were saddened and burdened in dealing with Dick's pain. Later that night, an idea began to take form in my thoughts. Soon the Spirit of joy began to bubble from within. The next night, I was on my way to the hospital dressed as a clown with a sign that read, "Hi, I'm your singing telegram." My daughter, Julie, and her friend, Gina, helped me create this awesome telegram. What a joy, Dick's spirit was lifted, and so was ours. That same joy touched the other patients in the intensive care unit. Going home that night, my husband introduced me to the toll man as Sonshine the Clown. Ron said that my name should be Sonshine spelled with "Son" because I let the love of Jesus shine through me.

I saw and felt in my spirit that night a broken, hurting world: a people that needed to know where their hope comes from. There was an empowering of my broken heart. I felt the love of Jesus and experienced the birth of Sonshine the Clown. In June of 1981, I enrolled in a clown makeup class. Soon, God helped me create a face and personality that is unique to Sonshine the Clown.

In 1983, our daughter Julie and I spent the summer in Europe doing some street clowning. While visiting my husband's family in Sweden, my mother died. Once more, I felt as if my heart could never love or give love again. I sent Sonshine's suitcase home to the United States with my husband Ron, feeling never again would I dress up as a clown. Sonshine was dead. During the next seven weeks, the Holy Spirit of God did a restoration on Sonshine and me that we were unaware of. Before leaving for Europe, I had made a commitment to march in the Libertyville Days parade. I was to be sponsored by a local merchant to promote his business. Julie and I returned home to the States on a Wednesday. The parade was on Saturday. I had made the commitment, so once more I felt obligated to dress up as Sonshine, even though my heart was breaking. The parade began at noon, and I was dressed as a clown but certainly was not very happy. As we walked the parade route, my friends, young and old, lined the sides of the street. I kissed and hugged and cried my way through Libertyville. God had planned a welcome home party for Sonshine and me. That day, I was unable to give my love, but the Lord was stretching my heart so I could receive love. There began that day, within Sonshine and me, a new awareness and desire to serve others. God began healing the intense pain I experienced in my mother's and father's deaths. The Spirit of the Lord spoke to my heart and said, "Go give my love to my people." God does have a plan for each of our lives, and it is a plan for good, not for evil.

Miss Phyllis

Sonshine the Clown

Sonshine the Clown

My first clown makeup class (1981)
Gina and Julie

CHAPTER 1

MY BIRTH

My parents were Lloyd and Minnie. I was born on December 3, 1940. There was much unrest in our world at that time. Our country was fighting a war in Europe. I was born on a farm in Forest City, Iowa. I was told that it was a very cold winter and that they had lots of snow that year. Within a few weeks of my birth, I developed pneumonia and became critically ill. My parents called the family doctor and asked if he would make a house call. The doctor said he would surely try, but the roads were bad. Before the doctor was able to get there, I had stopped breathing and began to turn blue. My father's older brother and sister lived with us on the farm. I am not sure who had the idea to put me in warm water and then cold water. By the time the doctor arrived, I was breathing again. The doctor had recently received a new drug named Sulfa. He gave the Sulfa drug to me, hoping it might heal me. My mother said it was a miracle drug and that it saved my life. I look back at all my life and know that it was Jesus that saved me. I have my little catechism book that was given to me when I was baptized. The date in my book of my baptism was January 12, 1941. Did my parents have me baptized before I became sick or after? That's a question I will ask them when I meet them in Heaven.

Ron, Mother, Julie

CHAPTER 2

OUR MOVE TO OTTUMWA, IOWA 1948

The Thompson family from Ottumwa, Iowa, would come north to go pheasant hunting each year. They stopped by our farm and asked if they could hunt on my father's land. My father agreed and also offered them bed-and-breakfast. They became good friends over the years that they hunted on our land. After the war was over, our country was experiencing hard times. The owners of the land we rented from were planning on selling the farm. Mr. Thompson told my father if he moved the family to Ottumwa, he could find him a job working for John Morell and Company.

In November of 1948, in a huge snowstorm, my father packed up his family. My mother, my brothers, Frank and Larry, and I were on our way south to Ottumwa, Iowa. We children had a pony named Bell who made the trip with us because of our many tears. My father's siblings, Almen and Olive, did not make the move with us; they found an apartment in Forest City. After three years of renting, my father found a small home he could buy for us. Life as I knew it was now very different. We were living in a big city of around twenty-five thousand people and growing. This was so different from the farm where I had lived and felt the security and peace of my family and friends. On the farm near Forest City, I had shared a room with my Aunt Olive. She would read the Bible to me every morning and every night. We would go to the neighbors for coffee and have delicious sweets, or they would come to our home. Now I was living in a place where no one talked about God, and everyone was mean-spirited.

One day, after the kids picked on me, calling me names, I ran to the vacant lot and hid in the weeds. I lay there looking at the sky, thinking how beautiful it was and missing my Aunt Olive. I began to cry out to God, telling Him how much I had been hurt. My tears became a song, and my heart felt like warm honey had been poured over my body. I began to sing, and then realized I did not understand the words that were coming out of my mouth. I felt a great love come over me. It would be years before I learned what had happened to me on that day.

Moved to Ottumwa Iowa (1948)
Larry, Frank, Phyllis

CHAPTER 3

JUNIOR HIGH CONFIRMATION

When I became old enough, my mother insisted I take the classes at church and be confirmed. I did not know another friend or anyone in my school that was going to church or was a Lutheran. After signing me up for the classes, I learned there were fourteen kids in the class, and I would be spending the next two years with them. They were from wealthy farms and lived in smaller towns around us. Most of them were related to each other in some way.

Within the first weeks, we had three other kids from my junior high school join the class. The four of us became a great support and friends to each other. Without one another, it would have been hard to complete our two years. One of the things expected of us was to visit other Walter League groups in different churches. This was fun, and we met some really neat kids.

I would memorize my scripture assignment and could recite it to someone and have no problem. When I got to church, I would be so intimidated and fearful I could not remember what I had memorized. On Palm Sunday, we were brought before the church and questioned. We were supposed to have instant recall of everything we had learned. The pastor said that if we did not answer his question by a show of hands, he would fail us. I really wanted my mother to be proud of me. This seemed to mean so much to her. She had even bought me a new white pair of shoes with a pink flower on the side. All my shoes had been hand-me-downs from my cousin, so this was very special, having new shoes. I was standing in line coming up the stairs from the basement of the church, praying. I was so fearful it was hard for me to breathe. Then I felt a warm feeling like something being poured over my head, and it began to run down my body. I remember feeling beautiful and very special. We filed in front of the church and took our seats. Some songs were sung, and then the pastor came forward and introduced each one of us. He then began his questioning. With each question he asked, my hand flew up. He just stared at me in shock. When he called on me, I recited my answer with perfection. I knew, and I think he knew, that this was a God thing. God had answered my prayers and had given me instant recall of what I had hidden in my heart and mind.

CHAPTER 4

FRESHMAN YEAR OF HIGH SCHOOL

In my freshman year of high school, I went to church with a friend. She and her family were attending an Assembly of God church. The music was very beautiful, nothing like I had ever heard before. When the guest pastor made the altar call, I wanted to go forward. Then he said that this week they were going to have a time for anyone that wanted to be baptized. This was very new to me; I thought that only babies were baptized. I really felt and wanted to be baptized that week. Many years later, Ron and I committed our lives to serving God and were baptized in a swimming pool in Zion, Illinois. When Ron came up out of the water, a huge butterfly landed on his shoulder, staying there a long time. Some years later, Ron and I were baptized in the Jordan River in Israel. A pastor on our tour who had served with Pastor Andy (who would later become my daughter Julie's father-in-law) baptized us. When Ron and I came up out of the water, a flock of fifty-plus doves circled around our heads and then landed in the trees. Our tour group on shore broke into a song, singing "Amazing Grace." We felt God's love, peace, and joy surround us as we embraced one another.

CHAPTER 5

MY HORSE ACCIDENT IN 1956

In my sophomore year in high school, we were invited to a friend's house to ride his horse. By the time it was my turn, it was beginning to get dark. As I was mounting the horse, someone jumped off the pickup truck. There were empty metal chicken crates in the back of the truck, and the crates made a huge crashing sound, frightening the horse. I had just begun to mount the horse and had one foot in the stirrup as I was holding on to the saddle horn. The frightened horse took off in a full gallop down the driveway onto the gravel road. The saddle slipped, and I was under the belly of the horse thundering down this gravel road. I knew this was a life-or-death ride, and I cried out to God. Fear left me, and a great peace came over me. A bright light shone on me under the horse's belly. My body was being whiplashed in all directions. My head was facing the back legs of this galloping horse. The hooves of the horse were within inches from kicking me in the head. I was becoming very weak as I struggled to keep my body from being kicked. I then heard a voice say, "Untwist your right leg and rest the heel of your foot on the edge of the stirrup. Okay, now put your left heel on the edge of the stirrup." It was a huge struggle for me because I had become so weak. I now had both heels of my feet resting on the stirrups. I was in a fetal position under the belly of this galloping horse. The voice spoke again and said, "Let go." "I can't," I cried. "I'm afraid." The voice said again, "Trust me, let go." The light was so bright, and that same peace returned to me. I closed my eyes, knowing I had no other choice, and I let go. When my body hit the hard gravel road, everything went numb. I watched as the horse galloped over me. I remember thinking it was like watching something in slow motion.

By now, it was dark, so the kids brought the car to where I lay. They drove me home, and I knew I was badly hurt. I remember very little of that ride home. When we arrived home and my mother learned what had happened, she called an ambulance. I went into a coma before the ambulance arrived and remained in the coma for three days. I had fractured my skull, and the doctors wanted to airlift me to Iowa City. They were told that I was not to be moved. By moving me, it could cause more blood vessels in my brain to burst. They were unable to tell at that time if I had any brain damage. My family and friends surrounded me in those weeks with their love and encouragement.

God brought healing to my body, but the fear of horses grew. I have had an unhealthy fear of horses since the accident. In 2012, I went to Northern Minnesota vacationing with my family. Everyone wanted to go trail riding up the mountain but me. I told Julie I did not want to go. She said the kids really wanted me to go with them. After a lot of encouragement, I finally agreed to face my fear and to take the trail ride with the family. My grandson, Edison, knew that I was fearful but did not know why. When we got down from the mountain trail, Eddy said, "Nonne, you just fought a dragon and you slew it." I did indeed; the dragon of the fear of horses was dead.

CHAPTER 6

MARRIAGE TO RON

After I graduated from high school in 1959, I moved to Chicago and found a job working for Wielboldt's Department Store in the blouse department. I rented a room at an elderly German lady's home. I believe Ron felt I would be safe and protected living with her. This home was only one bus ride from my work. Ron enjoyed concerts, plays, and nice restaurants. My life became full of new friends and wonderful new activities. Ron was a Chicago boy and loved to show me his city. Our wedding took place in Ottumwa, Iowa, the following third of September in the church I was confirmed in. We spent our honeymoon at Giant City State Park in Southern Illinois.

After finding a basement apartment that summer of 1960, I then began looking for a new job. I was hired by a company, Wells Manufacturing, in Morton Grove, Illinois. It was a long bus commute for me. I had to take two buses, and then I would wait for the company van at the end of the bus line. After a few weeks of working there, the head accountant befriended me and offered to pick me up at my first bus transfer. He said, "I go right by there every morning." This was a huge blessing, as the winters in Chicago were cold and snowy. His name was Glen Hefner, and he became my earth angel. I was hired as their switchboard receptionist. I felt this was a fancy job, and I loved it. It was in the early sixties, so we all dressed to the hilt; everyone wanted to look like the movie stars. I remember wearing my boots and carrying my high-heel shoes to work. I was the first person you met when you came through the front door. I really enjoyed my job and met some nice people. Ron and I became longtime friends with some of them.

One day, this young man came in and asked to see Glen Hefner. That was when the girls told me at lunch who he was. They said he was Glen's son and that he owned the Playboy Club in downtown Chicago. They told me a lot about Hugh Hefner—he certainly was nothing like his father. We moved into a larger apartment and rented the upstairs from our friends Shirley and Al. It was then that Loraine and Dick and their friends came into our life. We are all still friends today, and some of the group now live in Heaven. When I was expecting Julie, we bought a home closer to Ron's parents in Chicago. In 1968, Ron's friend told him that this home was for sale in Libertyville, Illinois. The home had two and a half acres of land with woods behind the mowed area. I was overjoyed and so happy to find a home with this much land. The town had only about eight thousand people when we moved into our home. It was a great place to make friends and raise our children. Ron was working for WGN broadcasting at that time. The last years of work for him were with BP Amoco in downtown Chicago on Michigan Avenue. We and our friends belonged to a group called The Saints. Our group would help at the theaters and Orchestra Hall concerts, wherever we were needed. I would meet Ron and our friends on Friday night, and then we would go out for dinner. Later, we would help out with plays and concerts that we had signed up for. Some places we would usher, and at other theaters we helped with concession stands. We helped them with anything they needed. This was a fun time in our lives.

It was our tradition to have our Swedish Christmas party each year. I also did a "Teddy Bear Christmas Tea" for my girlfriends each Christmas. We would have a large Fourth of July picnic each year as well. Our program on the Fourth of July would be to honor our country and the men and women who served our country. Our programs were always very moving with songs and testimonies. The year of the Gulf War, we had six yellow ribbons tied around the big elm trees out front. On the Fourth of July, the newspaper reporter came to the house. He covered the story of us cutting the ribbons down and singing, "God Bless America." When we had our thirtieth picnic, which was our last picnic, it was covered by the newspaper. There were lots of tears that day. The following year, we moved to Kentucky. Ron was an only child. His parents came from Sweden. I adopted his Swedish culture when we got married. I was the keeper of the things that were Swedish. Today Julie has that title. She is the keeper of the Swedish things.

When I moved to Minnesota, I began again remembering and embracing my German and Norwegian culture.

There is much more that could be written between these lines. As I look back over the years, I see the awesome memories and blessings of a marriage that God put together. I am thankful for God's faithfulness to us.

Ron and I on a boat in the Chicago harbor

CHAPTER 7

SHERRI LYNN—A GIFT FROM GOD

In 1961, our first child, Sherri Lynn, was born with a rare brain disorder called INDS. When she was three years old, she was placed in a research hospital in Chicago, Illinois. The specialists advised us not to have any more children. Our Jewish doctor said we were too young and encouraged us to have more children. Four years later, we had Julie Ann. Then three years later, Ronald Michael was born. I was a very concerned mother as I watched them develop through the first two years of their life. God has blessed us with two awesome children and seven grandchildren. In 2002, our sixth grandson, Jared, was born. He had INDS, the same disease as his Aunt Sherri had. Jared's short life helped researchers identify the gene that causes INDS. Jared died in August of 2017, and he is now in Heaven with Jesus.

When Sherri Lynn was nine years old, she passed into the arms of Jesus. When we went forward to view Sherri's body, my heart was racing. She was beautiful like an angel. While she was living, I could at times see pain on her face, but not now; it was peaceful. My mother said, "Do you want to touch Sherri's hands?" This was something they did in my mother's generation. I said, "I don't think I can."

I felt fear. My mother took my hand and laid it on Sherri's hand. Sherri's hand went from being ice cold to being warm under mine. Then I heard this beautiful music all around us. When I asked the others, no one had heard the music but me. I felt a great joy in my heart and knew this was a God thing.

I wrote the following letter on December 16, 1970. After I finished writing Aunt Olive this letter, I realized how many times I would be repeating myself in the letters I must write. I wrote:

> What I am writing about is a very pleasant memory. I don't want to repeat and mix up my present thoughts of yesterday. Sometimes, when we say things too often, it's our nature to see a little more than what actually was. This is something I want to avoid. Yesterday was an important day in our lives, and we wish to share it with you. Therefore, this letter will be copied and sent to all our friends and family. Sherri Lynn died December 13, 1970 at 3:00 a.m. at the age of nine. She was born June 8, 1961. The cause of her death was not the brain disease itself but double pneumonia. She was shown to us yesterday morning, December 15, around

eight-thirty in the morning. At her funeral at 10:00 a.m., Pastor Stanglen gave a very reassuring sermon. He had been with us at the beginning, and having him at the end was a blessing. Sherri really looked beautiful with a smile on her face. She projected peace into our hearts. After all her years of suffering, we have much warmth knowing Sherri has gone home to Heaven. This is the first day of our loss yet I feel no loss, but that once again Sherri is with us. Sherri wore a white lace dress with a pale yellow underslip. It was an A-line cut that Julie had picked out for her. She wore a heart-shaped gold locket her godmother had given her when she was baptized. The flowers on her casket were white and yellow baby mums and carnations. There was a white ribbon that read, "To our beloved Sherri." The casket was an octagonal shape covered in a white material. When they brought it out from the funeral home, it reminded me of a huge Christmas present. Her godmother sent a yellow rose bud pillow that remained with her. The large spray of flowers stayed on the graveside. I brought home a pink poinsettia plant, a brandy snifter of pink rose buds, and baby's breath. So you see, we didn't really leave Sherri at the gravesite—we brought her home with us.

I hope everyone will share our love and peace throughout the holiday and throughout the coming years.

Love as always,
Ron, Phyllis, Julie, Ronnie

As I look back over the years, this may have been the start of my first Christmas letters.

It was also the year I began my search for more of Jesus.

Sherry Lynn 6 months old (1961)

CHAPTER 8

SCUBA DIVE IN FLORIDA 1972

Ron and I had gone snorkeling with a dive group on a coral reef in Florida. That day was so perfect, and the ocean was very calm. We signed up with this tour company for the next day too. We were going to dive on the statue of Christ that was in the John Pennekamp State Park. When we arrived, we were told that there were not enough people that signed up and that our tour was canceled. The young man encouraged us to rent a small motorboat and go to the site alone. We wanted so much to dive on this statue, so Ron said, "Okay, tell me how to get there." We were not wise to the ocean; it can be your friend and turn quickly and be your enemy. This was not a wise decision; we knew little about boating and even less about the ocean. The young man said, "Just follow the mangroves, and when you see lots of boats you will know you're at the statue." We had hired the forest ranger's daughter to watch our kids, so we were ready to dive. We did not even consider that this might not be a good choice for us. There were a number of boats at the site, so Ron thought we should go a little beyond them. The first thing they told us in our scuba class was to never leave the boat alone. We were both so excited that we were only focused on getting suited up and diving in.

Once we had jumped in the ocean, I knew we were in trouble. We had gone beyond the reef and were now in the Gulf Stream. Within minutes, we were several feet from our boat. We tried to swim back to the boat, but the current was too strong. In less than five minutes, we could no longer see the boat. I began to panic and started screaming, and the more I screamed, the less hyperventilating I did.

When you panic, you are rational in your mind, but your heart races out of control. We knew with too much oxygen in our body we could pass out. Now we were both screaming, and the more we screamed, the more our hearts began beating at a regular beat. This all happened in a short period of time, but it felt like hours. There were three young men in a boat coming full power toward us. They said their friends were diving on the Statue of Christ and thought they heard someone screaming. I was so spent. It took all of them to pull me into the boat. It was a long distance back to our boat. We later looked for them back at the dive shop, but no one remembered them. "Angels around us!" Were they angels? Why did they leave their friends in the ocean alone? Why did they not have swimsuits on? Ron told many people about our experience that day on the ocean. He told them that he looked up to the Heavens and said, "Lord, you can't let us die on a beautiful day like this."

CHAPTER 9

AUNT OLIVE'S HEALING

My Aunt Olive called me from Forest City, Iowa, in 1973. She said she had a large mass on her thyroid. Her doctor wanted to remove it with surgery, and what did I think about that? Aunt Olive was eighty-eight years old and had a lot of health issues. I did not feel peace about her having surgery at her age. I told her my kids and I would drive up from Chicago and that we would take her to the doctor for her Monday appointment. We arrived at her home late Saturday afternoon, and we planned to take Aunt Olive to church on Sunday.

On Sunday mornings, she always watched the Oral Roberts TV show. Aunt Olive was sitting on a chair in front of the TV. Oral Roberts pointed his finger at the camera and said, "There is a little old lady sitting in front of the TV that has a large mass on her neck. She has been having a hard time swallowing her food. If this is you, reach out and claim your healing in Jesus' name." Julie, Ronnie, and I rushed over to her, and we laid hands on her neck as Oral Roberts prayed for her. We saw a miracle. The mass began to shrink, and Aunt Olive could swallow without pain.

The next day, we took Aunt Olive to her doctor's appointment. The doctor was amazed, I think totally shocked, that the mass was gone. He wondered if the pills he had given her for her thyroid had shrunk the mass. Aunt Olive responded with a strong, "No, it was God that healed me through the ministry of brother Oral Roberts."

Aunt Olive lived to be ninety-two years old always giving God the glory. She was a woman of faith and had the gift of giving. I was so honored to be at her bedside when she passed into Heaven. When I arrived, she asked me to sing. Her breathing became very shallow with longer intervals between each breath. I knew that very soon she would be seeing the face of Jesus. "Absent from the body, present with the Lord." (2 Corinthians 5:8)

My Aunt Olive opened her eyes and mouth, turning her head to the far left. She then began to slowly turn her head to the right, looking up toward Heaven. What I felt in my spirit as I watched her was the word *awesome*. The word *awesome* means something so beautiful there are no words to explain the beauty of it. There was so much power in that room when she passed. I looked at the clock—she entered Heaven at 10:25 p.m. The next day, when we were clearing out her room, I noticed the clock had stopped at 10:25. Her clock had stopped the minute Aunt Olive had left earth for Heaven.

When my time comes to make my journey from earth to Heaven, my Aunt Olive will be waiting for me. I am so thankful I had an Aunt Olive in my life to love and encourage me. "To God be the glory, great things He has done."

Picture of my Aunt Olive

CHAPTER 10

ARE TONGUES FOR TODAY?

Some months after Sherri Lynn's death, my peace with God felt distant. Ron and I began to search for that peace. I had lots of questions, like, "God, if you are a good God, why would you let a baby be born with any disease?" Our search led us to places I would not go today. God in his great love and mercy brought people into our lives to show us where our healing would come from. Ron's friend Danny was coming to Libertyville every Friday night to hear a man speak. He invited us to go with him, and we accepted. The people there all seemed so happy and friendly. The music was upbeat, and there were more than two hundred people in the gym. Following the music, they began to pray. I thought there were a lot of foreigners there because I did not understand what they were saying. As I watched them and listened, I became very fearful and said to Ron, "Let's go, I think these people are drunk and are devil worshipers." The speaker then began to read from the Bible: "They saw what seemed to be tongues of fire that separated and came to rest on each of them. All of them were filled with the Holy Spirit and began to speak in other tongues as the Spirit enabled them. These people are not drunk, as you suppose. It's only nine in the morning! No, this is what was spoken by the prophet Joel: In the last days God says, I will pour out my Spirit on all people. Your sons and daughters will prophesy, your young men will see visions, your old men will dream dreams. Even on my servants, both men and women, I will pour out my Spirit in those days, and they will prophesy." (Acts 2:3, 14 and 18) Ron and I got up, leaving the meeting quite disturbed by what we had seen and heard. Danny called us later, trying to explain what we had seen. He said that this was the beginning of a revival where God was drawing people back to a personal relationship with Him through the supernatural.

This began a new search for me. I set out to prove that tongues were from the devil, not from God. Within that year, I read and talked with everyone I could about tongues. My pastor, Gene, and his wife, Shirley, were of great help. I also called my Aunt Olive, and she said, "Phyllis, if it's in the Bible, then it's true." I can accept that it happened in the Bible, but is it true for today? The book that really opened up the truth for me was written by Dr. Sherrill, *They Speak with Other Tongues*. It's still in print today. He, like me, was searching to prove tongues were false and not of God, while walking along the ocean one night, God showed up, and Dr. Sherrill began to speak in tongues. One afternoon in January of 1975, I was sitting alone in my living room in Libertyville, Illinois. I said, "God, if tongues are real and it's part of you, then I want to speak in tongues." I sat in my chair very still, listening, and then I felt a song in my heart. I opened my mouth and began to sing in a language I did not know. It was so, so beautiful. I instantly had a flashback to when I was a young child in Iowa. I was lying in the weeds, missing my farm home and my Aunt Olive. I then sang songs that made all my pain and sadness leave me; it never happened again until now. I knew my search was over, tongues are real, and God wants a personal relationship with me. I began to praise, sing, and talk to God like He was my best friend. I knew that my life as I knew it would be changed forever. I continue today to use my prayer language and speak in tongues. It is my source of God's grace and peace in my life. My life changed that day, and I have never doubted God's love for me or that I am his child.

CHAPTER 11

STOLEN BIKE

In the late 70s, we gave Ronnie a dirt bike for his birthday. This bike was the joy of his life. Late that summer, he and his friend were out riding their bikes. They stopped at a 7–11 for a treat. When they came out of the store, they saw a pickup truck leaving the parking lot with Ronnie's new bike in the back of the truck. I called the police later to report the stolen bike. The police told me that there had been a number of new bikes stolen that week. They said the bike would probably be taken to the city and be given a new serial number, making it easy to resell the bike. They were sorry, but if they found the bike, they would contact me. I called my husband at work Ron told me later that he began to pray for Ronnie for peace, and then asked God to lead him to the bike. When he got into our town, he went to the 7–11 store and again asked God to show him where the bike was. Ron said he felt like someone got into the car with him and was giving him the direction he should drive. He ended up in a vacant lot that was near the railroad tracks, north of town. The weeds were more than knee high, and there were signs of trash all around. Ron felt a strong urge to get out of the car and walk into the weeds. As he walked, he saw signs that someone else had been there before him, for the weeds had been knocked down. A few feet into the weeds, there was Ronnie's new bike. I believe God sends his angels when we ask, and even when we don't ask. Our God knows our needs long before we do.

CHAPTER 12

TRIP TO SWEDEN 1978

We traveled to Sweden as a family to see Ron's aunt and uncle. While we were there, we crossed by ferry over to Finland and took a train to Helsinki. We then boarded a ship from Helsinki to Leningrad, Russia. When we were planning this trip in the States, I felt the Holy Spirit tell me to take Bibles to Russia. Julie was thirteen, and Ronnie was ten, and they knew I had the Bibles to be given away when we got to Russia. There were many people back home praying for our safety. They prayed that we could get through the passport check without them finding the Bibles. I had wrapped each Bible in gift paper so they looked like gifts. We got off the ship, and both days no one looked into my bag or checked us; we were just waved through. I watched as others were pulled out of line and checked. There were no other children on the cruise ship, and we had a family passport. Wherever we traveled in the seventies, there were few children traveling. Our family in Sweden did not want us to go to Russia. There had been many Christians arrested and jailed for no reason. They had no idea I was planning on carrying Bibles with us into Russia. I heard God's voice in the States and knew I must say yes. That trip, I believe, prepared me for a trip to China two years later.

Aunt Ragnhild and Julie in Swedish costume

CHAPTER 13

TRIP TO CHINA

It was spring of 1980. I flew to Hong Kong to carry Bibles into China. We joined a group in Hong Kong that carried Bibles and other Christian materials to the believers. We taped the materials to our bodies. The weight of the materials was heavy, and it became hard to walk or sit. Our team got on a train to China that took three long hours. We had shown up at the train station at different times and were told not to speak or make eye contact with one another. When we arrived in China, we had to go through their customs. Our small overnight cases had false bottoms where we had hidden the big heavy commentaries, and then we put our overnight clothes and toiletries on top. We were told that if we were stopped, we were to say we were traveling alone for pleasure.

My thoughts went back to Russia and how God had protected me and my family. I also remember reading how God had protected Corrie Ten Boon years ago. My heart was beating so fast I felt like I might pass out. I could see others that were in line and those that were on the other side. When I got to the front, the man never looked up; he just waved me through.

That was not the case with other teams that went to China months later. We were told that when we arrived at the hotel, we were not to say anything regarding our trip. The rooms were all bugged. We were all to be tourist travelers, so we played that part well. We ate in a fine restaurant and went sightseeing. When we arrived back in Hong Kong, we were all praising God for his faithfulness. From China, we went to Singapore and then to Malaysia. In each country, we were cared for by Christians living there. At that time, you could be arrested for sharing the Gospel with anyone. We ministered in house groups, sharing the Bible and giving our personal testimonies. It was amazing to see so many doors open to us to share the Gospel. I believe this experience helped me to have the faith to travel some years later alone to the Philippines.

CHAPTER 14

HEALING OF JULIE'S WART

The summer of 1982, a group of us from church attended an Aldersgate conference in Des Moines, Iowa. My daughter Julie had this huge wart on her thumb for weeks. We had tried different kinds of remedies, but nothing would heal it. Julie's junior prom was the following weekend, and she wanted this wart gone. The last night of the conference was going to be a healing service. During the meeting, they asked those that needed prayer to come to the front. The lady that was going to pray for us talked to Julie about the wart. She lovingly took Julie's hand, and very gently began to rub the wart. She said, "We are not going to curse this wart off. We are going to love it off." She began praying for Julie, all the time so gently rubbing Julie's wart. There was so much power from that love prayer over Julie's wart. She ended the prayer asking for Julie's thumb to be restored and healed. As we got ready to leave, she told Julie to keep gently rubbing the wart and thanking God for a healthy thumb. Within hours, you could see it becoming pink, and the crusty skin was starting to come off. After a few days, the wart was gone. Julie went to her junior prom without a bandage or wart.

The message for us was that we were to love the unlovely. By loving the unlovely, we would be able to see the lovely come forth. That was a huge blessing to all of us who had attended the conference. It is something that I remind myself to do whenever I face the unlovely things in life. If we will learn to love the unlovely, the lovely will come forth. God's healing power is still at work for us today.

CHAPTER 15

VISION OF MOTHER 1983

Julie and I planned a two month trip to Europe to visit Ron's family and then end our trip in the United Kingdom. My mother became very ill, and I was quite concerned that she might die while we were on our trip. Lisa, my niece, brought Mother to Chicago to spend a few days with us before we left on our trip. I spoke to my mother about my concerns for her health issues. She said, "Phyllis, you have had your plans made for months. I think you should make the trip with Julie just as you planned." That night when I was alone, I cried out in total pain to God, "Oh, Father God, I am so afraid to leave the States for Europe. I cannot bear to be alone in Europe if my mother should die while I am there."

Everything began to change around me, and I became aware of standing in the middle of a southeastern Arizona desert. I was looking to the north at a huge mountain range with very tall peaks.

In my vision: I saw this huge, gigantic tree. I sat down leaning against the tree. I felt someone squeeze in between me and the tree, and then he began to massage my neck and back. The person massaging me began to speak to me. "I know you have concern that your mother might die while you're in Europe. Look up at the mountains where the two peaks come together. Are they not absolutely beautiful and so very awesome? Now look at the sunset beginning on the far west side of the mountain range." The sunset was very brilliant, yet I was able to look deep into the contrasting colors of the sunset. The voice drew my attention back to the sunset. "Look! Watch!" I did and the sunset went down behind the mountain peaks and disappeared. I felt a heavy, great sadness and cried again. It was so beautiful, and now it was gone. The voice spoke once again and said, "Look up!" The sun was now rising beyond the other mountain peak, and it was more intense in beauty than the first sunset. The voice said, "When your mother dies, she will rise on the other side of the mountain more alive there than she is alive today."

I called my brothers and told them of my vision. I said, "If Mother dies while I'm in Europe, you must know she is with Jesus, and we will see her alive again." Because of this vision, I was able to stay in Sweden and minister to Ron's family, who were grieving loved ones. The Spirit spoke to my heart saying that my concern should now be for the living. My mother was now in Heaven with Jesus. I felt that this would also include finishing my trip with my Julie as planned. It was a difficult decision to make. During our final days in Sweden, God brought healing to my heart. Julie and I finished our tour through the United Kingdom. We arrived home in time to prepare Julie for her first year of college. She began her new life at St. Olaf College late that summer of 1983. My mother has never seemed dead to me. The vision God gave me made her alive in my heart then, and she still remains alive in my heart today. I have learned over these years to walk by the Spirit and not by the flesh. I am so very thankful!

CHAPTER 16

THE CAR THAT SPUN IN CIRCLES

In the middle of 1980s, my friend Sylvia and I were driving to Southern Illinois to her college reunion. We were driving about sixty miles an hour; the traffic was not heavy. The car in front of us began to spin around in circles. We were on a two-lane road, so it spun into both lanes. Both of us cried out at the same time to Jesus. I said, "Lord, help us," and Sylvia said, "Oh, sweet Jesus." All the cars and trucks came to a stop. Miracle of miracles that not one vehicle hit another. The car in front of us, that had spun out, came to a stop, facing us in the wrong direction. It was only two feet from our car. The young woman looked at us in horror and then covered her face and began to weep. All the trucks and cars began to straighten out and move forward up the road. I believe that when we cried out to God, he sent his angels of protection, keeping us safe. I have had the privilege of seeing my guardian angel working overtime in my life to keep me safe. I write my stories with a thankful heart.

CHAPTER 17

RONNIE'S PILOT LICENSE

My husband, Ron, received his private pilot license in the nineteen seventies. He would often take our son Ronnie flying with him. When Ronnie was five years old he announced that he was going to be a pilot someday. He was going to own his own airport and fly us all over the world. When Ronnie was thirteen, his father found an instructor who would work with him. They gave Ronnie a log book, and they settled on three or four lessons a year. They felt this would keep his interest in flying alive. Ronnie was too short then to see out the window of the plane, so he would carry a pillow to his lessons. On his 16th birthday in 1984, Ronnie took his driver's test to get his auto license. Later that same day, the weather cleared, and he soloed in the airplane. Now he needed to practice his touch-and-go's. One weekend I was washing my kitchen floor on my hands and knees. I felt a huge, heavy burden come into my heart. I stretched out on the floor and began to sob. I cried and prayed in tongues for a very long time. Finally the burden lifted, I dried my eyes and finished washing the floor.

Later that day Ronnie came home. One look at him and I could tell something was very wrong. He told me that when he was practicing his touch-and-go's, another plane came into his airspace. As his plane began to climb, this other plane flew in front of him making a landing. One's first instinct is to pull back on the throttle to miss the plane in front of him. If Ronnie would have done that, he would have stalled the plane and crashed. He was a 16 year old, new pilot, with little experience then. God gave him the insight to push forward on the throttle giving the plane more power and lift. He was then able to climb above the incoming plane. It was a close call. I asked him at what hour of the day this happened? He checked his log book. It was the very hour I was on my face praying.

My son, Ronnie and I loved night flying. We would leave the Waukegan, Illinois airport and follow Lake Michigan to downtown Chicago to Meigs Field. We would get a coke, then when the lights of the city starting coming on, we would get in the plane and follow the shoreline back to Waukegan. This is a wonderful memory I have of flying in small planes with Ronnie. When Ronnie was ready to practice his sod field landing, he asked me to go along with him. We flew to some farmer's field in Wisconsin. The sod runway was cut through the middle of the farmer's field. Our landing was no problem. It was very rough and bumpy as we expected it to be. Ronnie turned the plane around, and we were ready for take off. We were now taking off down this sod runway full throttle but nothing seemed to be happening. We were not getting any lift on the plane. There was a line of tall trees at the end of this runway that we had to clear. The trees were getting closer and closer: and my heart was in my throat. I prayed silently, "Lift us Lord, lift us." I looked at Ronnie, his face was set in a firm expression. His hand was pushing forward hard on the throttle but nothing was happening. I kept praying, "Please Lord, give us lift." The trees were fast approaching us. Ronnie never wavered. He held that throttle forward. Then the plane popped up like a jumping frog, and we began to lift. We cleared those trees by only a few feet. We both began to scream at the same time, "We made it, we made it!" We were praising God at the top of our lungs. I believe we popped over those trees with supernatural help. Were our guardian angels again at work protecting us? Ronnie was always focused and had a natural ability for flying. He has flown for different airlines, large and small, to get his air hours. When Ron's son, Mitchell, was four years old, Ron took him flying along the coast of Florida. Mitchell has now graduated from college with an aviation degree. He has completed his Certified Flight Instructor, Multi-Engine Commercial Rating, Instrument Rating, First Class Medical, Commercial Drone Pilot. He just finished his commercial rating. In August of 2017, Mitchell took me flying down the Ohio river. I was one of his first passenger's after he had made his first solo flight. On December 26, 2019, I was Mitchell's first student to receive a flying lesson in the right seat. The day was perfect: it was 61 degrees in Kentucky. What an awesome memory I have. Thanks Mitchell! That was a huge honor and privilege for me. I pray always that the angels be sent to protect Mitchell as he pursues aviation as his career.

Ron giving Mitchell right seat time

Nonne's first Solo with Mitchell

CHAPTER 18

YOU NEED ANTIFREEZE?

It was the year 1996, Ron and his friend, Bill, were in Chicago for a Promise Keepers conference for men. I had scheduled ministry on the South Side of Chicago that same weekend. Ron wore many different hats in our ministry, and being my driver was one of them. He did not want me going to the South Side of Chicago alone. Bill's wife, Shirley, said she would go with me. Bill and Shirley were fairly new Christians and really wanted to learn more about God. Pastor and Barb Perkins had opened a mission house in the burned-out part of South Chicago. This was my third time to bring my full Gospel message to this neighborhood. This was not a safe place at night. Even during the day, you needed to be careful. In the past, we had seen many salvations and healings. There were volunteers from Pastor's church that came out to make a huge barbecue picnic for everyone. It was a big deal for that poor neighborhood. We saw druggies receive Christ, and God touched the hearts of children of all ages. The day was extremely hot, and after my program, I was weary. God had blessed all of us, and now I was so ready to go home.

We had gotten a few miles up the road on the expressway when my car light went on indicating overheating. I knew the exit I was getting off on was not real safe, but I didn't feel I had a choice. As we pulled up to the light, it went red. When I stopped, my car died. I got out of the car but could not get anyone to stop to help us. Keep this in mind, I was dressed in my Sonshine the Clown costume, and people were afraid of me. The light changed, and a young man in a truck had to stop for the light. I leaned into his open window and begged him to help Shirley push the car out of harm's way across the street. He felt sorry for me and agreed. Now my car was across the street on a frontage road. The car was steaming. He said we would need antifreeze. He told us there was a gas station around the corner, to get into his truck, and that he would take us there. The three of us squeezed into his truck, and off we went. The computer was down at the gas station, so they were not going to sell me any antifreeze. I pleaded with the young man. "Please take my ten dollars and keep the change." He accepted. Praise God, we now had our gallon of antifreeze. When we returned to our car, the young African American man poured the antifreeze into our radiator. He stood back, shaking his head, saying we needed another gallon of antifreeze. I looked at Shirley and then back at the young man. It was one of those moments that screamed, *What now?*

Out of nowhere, a white van came around the corner. The side door flew open, and a young Spanish lady said,

"Do you need antifreeze?" As she handed me a gallon of antifreeze, I said, "Antifreeze?" I took the antifreeze and handed it to Shirley. Shirley handed it to the young man. We looked at each other, and then we looked down the road, and there was no van in sight. I had said it was a frontage road. It was a straight, long frontage road, and there was nothing on it. We were stunned and wordless. The young man put the antifreeze into the radiator. I tipped him, and we said goodbye. All the way home, Shirley and I tried to rationalize what had just happened to us. Bottom line, we were sure that we had encountered angels. We had a good hour's drive to get back to Libertyville. When I turned the engine off in the garage, the car would not start again. When Ron got home, he said that the water pump had broken. It was a miracle for our car to run as far as it did without a water pump. I believe God gave us that experience to show us how He uses His angels in our life to help us. Angels are always around us we just don't always see them actively working for us.

CHAPTER 19

TOUR OF ISRAEL

The year was 1991. My friend Maureen and I were going on a mission trip to Israel with Pastor Gerald. His daughter, Joanne, and her husband would be leading our worship time. We were to end our stay in Jerusalem, attending the Christian Embassy Conference and celebrating the Feast of Tabernacles at the Hilton Hotel.

We saw the hand of God and his protection in each village we visited. At one of the village home churches that we visited, we were to encourage the new believers. One of the uncles was so angry that his nephew had received Christ that he poisoned his baby's milk. The family and new believers prayed, and the baby was miraculously healed. The man was so convicted that he repented and became a believer. Because of this, other people in this little village received Christ. The people in this village church were Palestinians and all new believers. The word had gotten out that we were in Israel, and so they invited us to visit their home church. During our worship time, a message was sent to us that we must leave and leave now. As we drove away, we saw the children and older people gathering rocks down the street to throw at our bus. As we left the village, we could feel the evil, yet we rejoiced in the awesome grace of God and His protection.

That night, we stayed in a small hotel owned by a Christian family near the Sea of Galilee. Jesus had visited some Palestinians from the Golan Heights in a dream. They were told that Pastor Gerald was in this hotel, and he would tell them all about Jesus. There was a bounty on Gerald's head at this time, so we were all somewhat anxious about the meeting. The believers invited the Palestinians to join us for a time of fellowship. When they arrived, no one was sure what would happen. The air felt charged, and I remember my heart was racing fast. There were six of them that had come down from the Golan Heights. When they came into the room, they embraced the other brothers and cried. You could feel the fear leaving and joy being replaced as everyone began thanking God for his supernatural visitation to these brothers. After we had dinner, we sang songs and worshiped the Lord, thanking him for what he was doing in Israel.

We spent our last week in Jerusalem attending the Christian Embassy Conference. The first night at the Hilton Hotel, the Israeli prime minister was there to welcome us. Randy was the choreographer of the dance and worship for the conference. It was awesome. We were worshipping God with Christian people from all over the world. A German pastor took the pulpit and asked the Jewish people to forgive his people for the Holocaust. It was a powerful time of forgiveness and tears. This pastor really set the tone for the anointing and forgiving power of God for the conference.

Qumran Caves

On one of our nights, we had dinner in the desert at the Qumran Caves where the Dead Sea Scrolls were found. Our night began with the shofar being blown. Then the dancers and musicians performed for us on the rocks under spotlights. It was magical, absolutely beautiful under the starry night sky. There was an anointing that surrounded all of us. We are told that each one of us have our own guardian angel. I wondered that night how many other angels God sent to protect us in the middle of the desert. You could feel God's hedge of protection around us. A memory that will live on forever in my heart.

Paraded Down the Streets of Jerusalem

On Wednesday, there was a parade organized down the streets of Jerusalem in order to bless the Jewish people. This was the only time we were told that we could reach out and have contact with an orthodox Jewish Rabbi. We lined up according to our country. In front of us was the state of Oklahoma. They were dressed as Native Americans. Maureen and I were among the people from the state of Illinois. We had planned that our costumes would be white dresses with a wide sash of red, white, and blue that read, "American Ambassador." Our sash went over our head and hung down the right side of our dress. We wore tiaras on our heads and carried baskets of candies. We would give to the adults the American flag pin and candy to the children along the parade route. There had to be more than one hundred Americans blessing the Jewish people. In total, there might have been a thousand people from all the other countries. At the end of the parade route, a journalist from the *Jerusalem Post* asked Maureen and I if he could interview us. President Bush was in talks at that time, seeking peace agreements in Israel. They wanted to know how we felt about what was being negotiated for the Jews. I remember saying, "Lord, please fill my mouth and give me what I should say." We commented something like this, "We respect and support our president in what he does. However, God has given this land to the Jewish people, and this land will forever belong to the Jewish people."

Our Invite to Tea

On our tour, the cameraman befriended us, inviting us to visit his family and mother-in-law for tea. We had spent the day before having lunch with his wife in Jerusalem. She now wanted us to meet her mother. We thought "how sweet," so we accepted the invitation. He and his driver picked us up one night after dinner. We drove east toward the Mount of Olives, and when we started down the other side of the mountain, everything changed. The roads were no longer paved; the housing was poor and crowded. We pulled up in front of a small house. His wife and children and mother-in-law welcomed us. They served us tea and some sweets. His wife's English was good, and she translated to her mother all during our fellowship. Then there was a knock on the door, and a man told us we must leave right away. We were ushered to the car with short goodbyes. Keep in mind we were once again in a Palestinian neighborhood. When we were leaving the area, the driver was driving very fast. We rounded a corner where men and boys were gathering. Our car flew past them, leaving them in a cloud of dust. We were told that these men meant us great harm. They had received word we were visiting there. I asked them, "Who was the man that warned us of danger?" No one seemed to know who the man was. It was unclear to everyone. Was he the angel of the Lord watching over his naive children? The next day, our host left a beautiful gift for both Maureen and I at the front desk. His note said, "Thank you for blessing my family. I wanted them to meet godly Christians."

Lunch at the Abbey

While we were in Jerusalem, we made contact with a group of believers both Jewish and Palestinian. This meeting needed to take place in secret for the safety of all. The Greek Orthodox Church gave us a room where we could meet and have lunch together. We all sat on the floor, eating from a huge round tray. We were to eat with our left hand this traditional meal. We were so blessed that this would have been the way Jesus would have eaten His meals. You would take a hand full of crust then squeeze it until it formed a pocket around the rice, meat, and veggies. It was very tasty. This was a very different way of eating for all of us. We all felt bonded to our new family in Christ. After singing and some dancing, we said our goodbyes. What we had experienced would always be locked in a moment of time. We all felt, as we left the Abbey, that we had been on holy ground.

Our Bedouin Camp Visit

Our group was invited to the desert to visit with a nomadic tribe of people. The chieftain's granddaughter had become a believer while attending college in the States. She wanted us to share Jesus with her family and tribe. This was a very beautiful meeting, one-of-a-kind experience for all of us. Everyone was in their traditional dress and so gracious, inviting us into their large tent. We were served coffee and different kinds of sweets and fruits. The chief said he had more than one wife but was looking for another one. He asked our leader if he could buy Maureen for his wife. He said that he would offer camels, goats, gold, anything that we wanted for his new bride-to-be. Our leader thanked him very graciously, saying this was a great honor to Maureen and to our group. He explained she had a husband in the States and was very happily married to one man. Our chieftain laughed. I think he was just making some jest and humor for all of us. We were truly entertained and loved by all. They asked us lots of questions about our faith. We were really blessed during the time we spent with them. As we left our new friends, we passed a UN truck coming down the road. They would have had a lot of questions for us to answer if we would have been at the Bedouin Camp. Everywhere we visited we felt the peace and protection of God. There was no doubt in my mind that there were angels all around us.

CHAPTER 20

MY FREE DAY AT CONFERENCE

I read a book *Blood Brothers* by Father Elias Chacour from I'billin, Galilee, Israel. He had opened a school for Christians, Palestinians, and Jewish children so they could be taught and educated. I was so impressed with his story. I wrote, asking him if I could give my full Gospel program to the children of his school when I was in Israel. He called me in the States and was delighted that I would want to do this. His school is Mar Elias Education Institutions. He has now a long-awaited Arab Christian Israeli University. On my free day of our conference, I took a bus to Tel Aviv. From there I was to catch a bus to I'billin. Maureen and I had walked in the parade the day before. We had been interviewed by a journalist from the *Jerusalem Post*.

Now as I waited for the bus, I saw a photo of Maureen and me on the front page at the newsstand. I bought two papers and went far away from the people to read the article. We were definitely described as Christians here to bless the Jewish people. I finally got on the bus headed deep into Palestinian territory. After an hour on the bus, English was no longer on the road signs. Over the next forty-five minutes, the bus had only a few people left on it. I had no clue where I was and could not read any of the signs. I went to the front to ask the bus driver if he would tell me when we arrived in I'billin. The driver could not speak English. That's when I was aware of a man sitting behind the driver. He assured me that when we arrived at the little town, he would tell me. I thanked him and went back to my seat.

I began praying, "God, you have brought me this far. I have no one else I can trust. You have to show me how I can get to this school and get me there safe." Soon we came to this very small town. The streets were dirt roads with only a few stores and houses. The bus stopped in front of a coffee shop to let me off. I had been given a telephone number, so I went inside the shop to use their phone. No one in the shop spoke English. My thoughts were "Lord, now what?" In walked a young girl. She came right up to me and asked if I was an American. I said yes that I was, and I needed to reach Father Chacour.

She said, "Please let me help you. I know all about his school." She asked the lady serving coffee for her phone and made the call to the school. She gave the phone to me. I began telling the school secretary my name and that I had arrived. She said she would send a driver to pick me up. I thanked her and hung up. When I turned around, the young girl was gone. My car came for me and took me to Father Chacour where I had lunch with a group of visitors. I was then taken to the school where I performed my Gospel program. I was well received by the students and teachers. They were very kind to me. I don't think they had ever seen a person put on full-clown makeup. Some of them had never seen a clown before. Once I got into full costume, I preformed my Gospel show for the students and staff.

It's a wonderful memory that will live in my heart forever. Father Chacour then drove me to Bethlehem. From there, I had only one bus back to Jerusalem. God's hand of protection was on me. The group leaders did not want me to make that trip. They felt it was not safe. I knew that God had orchestrated this assignment while I was in the States. I had to trust Him and go. Maureen was in prayer for me all day. Looking back, I wonder, was the man on the bus or the young girl an angel? If not, they were my earthly angels, without them I would have been lost.

CHAPTER 21

I LEFT THE TOUR GROUP

I said my goodbyes to my tour group and friend Maureen. We had shared so many wonderful experiences together on this trip to Israel. I was leaving the tour now to spend the next four days with my friend Judith from Tel Aviv. Judith had come to Illinois with Friendship Force; we had been her host family in the States. She had now invited me to spend time with her and her family in her country. Her son Ron was in charge of a kibbutz in the Golan Heights area. I took a cab to the large bus terminal in Jerusalem where I boarded a bus for Tel Aviv. I had two large suitcases because of my clown props and costume. I was struggling to keep all things together. A young man came up to me asking if he could help me to get on the bus. I thanked him and said, "Yes." It was very crowded, and I really needed his help. He took a seat next to me and asked me where I was going. He seemed interested in all the things that I saw and did on my tour. The bus began to empty out and soon it was just him and me. My friend Judith said she would pick me up at the end of this bus line. She also made a point that if she was not there, to wait and not get into anyone's car. When we arrived at the end of the line, Judith was not there waiting for me. The young man helped me get my luggage off the bus. He was concerned that Judith was not there waiting for me. He told me "Do not accept a ride from anyone you don't know." As we were saying our good-byes, Judith pulled up to the curve. You could see she was visibly concerned that there was a man with me. She later said it was not safe to be a woman alone in this neighbor-hood. The next day we drove up to the Golan Heights to Judith's sons' home at the kibbutz. When you drive through these little Palestinian towns everyone knows from your car license what nationality you are. Judith warned me that the children may throw rocks at our car. We also had to cross a long, high concrete bridge to get to the kibbutz. On the east side was a stretch of land called nomad's land. On the other side of this land strip was Syria. If there was any shooting, she said we would wait behind the large con-crete walls till the shooting stopped. Then we would make a mad run for the hills. All went well. We had no problems going or coming or any other incidents. Our time at the kibbutz was great fun. We met people from all over the world that were staying at the kibbutz. On our free day we went swimming at a hot mineral springs over looking the Syrian Valley. While we were there, ambulances from different towns in Israel came with very sick people. They would carry the people from the ambulances on stretchers with their clothes on. Then they dipped them into the hot, bubbly, mineral waters. They would then put them back into the ambulance still wet and leave. There was a line of ambulances waiting for their turn. This felt like something Jesus might have experienced when He walked the land. Why is it that angels seem to show up more when I am out of the country. The Holy Spirit said, "That's because you are in need and ask God for His help. When you are not in a crisis you feel you can do it all by yourself." My prayer is now, "Lord show me your angels. Make me aware of them every day." Was the man on my bus an angel? Did God blind the children's eyes to our Jewish license plate number? Were the men in Syria taking a coffee break when we crossed the bridge? I don't know. I am just thankful that I know this, "If God is for me, who can be against me."

Maureen and I interviewed by the Jerusalem Post in Israel

CHAPTER 22

MY FIRST MISSION TRIP TO THE PHILIPPINES

My first trip to the Philippines was in 1997. I went to minister in four Bible schools that Billy had started in remote areas on the islands. We joined the staff in teaching the youth camps during the days. The nights were open to the public. We had music and testimonies, and then I would give my full Gospel program. Many people came down out of the mountains when they heard a clown would be there performing. I saw people of all ages give their hearts to Jesus. The local pastors, following my program, would invite people to come forward for prayer. There were lots of healings, and people were delivered from evil spirits and witchcraft. These villages had witch doctors, and unless you pleased them, they would put curses on the people. We saw the power of God break the curses off the people, and they became free.

On the island of Davao, the rains came early. We were on our way by bus coming over the mountains. As we came over the mountain through the jungle, our bus got stuck in the mud. The bus was piled high with suitcases, so high, I thought we would tip over. Two tall, white men stood in front of the bus and said, "I want all of you men to get off the bus and start pushing the bus." We had been sitting there a good ten minutes, and not one man had moved. Now all the men jumped up, got off the bus, and started pushing. When we got to the top of the little rise, looking back, the ruts were two to three feet deep. We were then told this was going to be our pit stop, so everyone got off the bus. People scattered everywhere to find their tree to hide behind. When we got back on the bus, I looked for the two white men to thank them. No one knew where they had gone or who they were. I never saw them again. I believe God had sent us angels in our need.

The bus that got stuck in the Philippines

CHAPTER 23

ANGEL CAME TO RON

By April of 2003, Ron had become bedridden. The Lewy body disease was progressing, and he was unable to speak. One morning when he woke up, he began to talk to me about this angel he had seen. He told me, "Phyllis, a very tall angel came here last night." I was so excited he was talking I started asking him questions. I asked, "What did the angel want?" Ron said, "The angel came to help you." I responded, "Great, I sure do need help." I asked Ron whether the angel was a male or female angel. He replied, "Phyllis, you know angels do not have a sex." Ron never spoke again after that; he passed within the month. This happened sixteen years ago, and I have never felt fear of being alone, because I have an angel that lives with me.

That fall, I had some friends stay with me. Lois asked me the next morning if I knew that I had an angel living in my home. She said that the angel she saw was very tall. I told her that Ron had the vision of the angel moving into our home before he died. Our granddaughter Brikken brought to Popa's memorial her praying bear, Beanie Baby, for me. I set it on my dresser in my bedroom; it brought much comfort to me.

A year or more after Ron had passed, when I was dusting in my bedroom, I picked up my praying bear and noticed it had a name tag on it. I read the tag. The angel's name was Hope. I knew in my heart at that moment that the angel living with me was the Angel of Hope.

CHAPTER 24

MY DREAM OF RON 2003

I had a dream within the first six months after Ron had died. In my dream I was walking in this huge crowd of people. I had a sick feeling that I had lost Ron. He was no longer with me. I was scanning the crowd for him. I saw a man in the crowd that had a left shoulder a little lower than his right. I pushed my way through the crowd to reach him. I was sure it was Ron. It was not my Ron. The next thing I remembered, I was rushing into the Frontier Hotel in Las Vegas. I asked the lady at the front desk if Ron was checked in there. The desk attendant shook her head sadly and said Ron had left a few days ago. "I am so sorry," she said. In my dream, I was now in the Grand Canyon at the El Tovar Hotel. I remember running in, very distressed, asking if Ron was there. The desk clerk said, "No, he had been there but had left earlier." I began to walk around the rim of the canyon looking for Ron. I sat down on a stone near the canyon edge and began to cry. Then I felt the Lord in my dream say to my heart, "Phyllis, Ron is no longer here on earth. He is with me. You must stop looking for him wherever you go." That dream was the beginning of my grief journey. I knew then that my life as I knew it would never be the same. My Ron would no longer be a part of my physical life here on earth.

The first few years of Ron's illness, we were still able to travel to Europe with Dick and Lorraine. I always held Ron's hand so he would not wander off. At the Tulip Festival in Holland, Dick had taken Ron to the bathroom. Lorraine and I were outside waiting for them. In front of us was a three foot stone wall. Dick was standing on the wall looking over the crowd, and we felt that Ron had wandered off. We watched and knew that Dick had spotted Ron in the crowd. He got down off the wall, walked over, and took Ron's hand. Dick continued to hold Ron's hand to keep him safe on our trip. It brings tears to my eyes as I remember the sweet love Dick had for my Ron. The blessing was, we never lost Ron. We hung on to Ron's hand just like God hangs on to us.

Trip to Tulip Festival in Holland
Dick, Lorraine, Phyllis, Ron

Ron's face in the clouds

CHAPTER 25

RON'S FACE IN THE CLOUDS

Shortly after my husband Ron had died, I went to our condo in Florida. I drove to Venice, Florida to visit my friend Pat for the weekend. Our girls, Gina and Julie, started kindergarten together so Pat knew my family well. Pat and I were taking chicken soup to Pat's sick friend. As we started to back out of the driveway Pat cried out, "Look, Phyllis, there's Ron in the clouds." The image looked like Ron would have looked twenty-five years ago with his full beard. We sat there and watched, amazed. As the clouds began moving, the image of Ron disappeared. I said, "Pat, did we really see Ron in the clouds?" She said, "Phyllis, it was Ron." I called Kristi, my daughter-in-love who lived in Kentucky, the next day and told her what we saw. She said that on their way to church Saturday night, Mitchell was so excited yelling, "Popa's in the sky, stop the car!" He was only about four years old at that time.

Back in Louisville, my friend Susan was painting a mural in my master bathroom to look like Tuscany, Italy. She had finished the clouds in the sky, then got off the ladder to check her work. She stood in the doorway to see if there should be more clouds added. When she looked up to the ceiling she saw a face in the clouds and thought it was Jesus. Susan panicked and left my house that day. She called me later wanting to know when I would be returning home. I told her I would be home by the weekend. She said, "Call me when you get into town, I want to meet you at your house." I just thought she had finished the bathroom and wanted to see my reaction to the mural. When I got home she was sitting in her car and seemed uptight. She led me straight into the house to the bathroom. I stood in the doorway of the bathroom and looking towards the ceiling, I saw the face of Ron and started to cry. It was the same image of the face of Ron that Pat, Mitchell, and I had seen two weeks before. Susan had never met Ron or even seen a picture of him. I found the picture of Ron from our Alaskan cruise when he had his full beard. There was no doubt, it was Ron's face in the clouds; on the left side of his mouth, his lip turns up a little. It was a perfect image of Ron in the bathroom clouds. I was in a grief class at that time and many of the people were having dreams of their loved ones. I had prayed, "Please Lord, help me with my grief. Let me have a dream or show me something to help me in my healing process." My prayer was answered. Susan and I cried and praised God for His love and compassion toward me. Ron and I had wanted to spend time in Tuscany when we retired. I began every day in the Spirit, thanking God for all His blessings and my wonderful memories of Ron and our travels. It was a miracle! I spent my mornings preparing for my day, and nights ending my day in my Tuscany bathroom with Ron looking down at me. God 's comfort to me at that time was like wrapping me in a warm blanket.

I lived in that condo in Kentucky for twelve more years. Whenever someone new came to visit me, I would show them the image of Ron in the clouds in my bathroom. They would always gasp seeing the face of Ron looking down at them. Then I would show them the picture of Ron from our Alaskan cruise. There was no doubt the image in the clouds was Ron. As we searched the clouds, we also identified angels, a dove, and the cross. My God understood my pain. He knew what it would take to bring His grace and healing power into my life. I moved to Minnesota in 2015 to be near my daughter Julie and her family, leaving my mural in Kentucky. I often shut my eyes and my mural comes into focus, and I am once more under the Tuscany sun with my sweet Ron. I am so blessed and highly favored.

PRINCESS CRUISES   STAR PRINCESS   *THE LOVE BOAT™*

Ron and I on our Alaskan cruise

CHAPTER 26

THE RING GOD PUT ON MY FINGER

My dear sweet Ron passed into Heaven in June of 2003. That fall I joined a grief class at South East Church in Louisville, Kentucky. The first statement our group leader Betty made was, "The world will tell you that you won't get over this loss. I'm telling you through the power and grace of God you will." Months later Betty gave me a book "Redeeming Love" by Francine Rivers. This book is a powerful retelling of the Bible story of Hosea. The setting of this book is in California gold country in 1850. It was a time when men sold their souls for a bag of gold, and women sold their bodies for a place to sleep. The story is about a young girl named Angel who was sold into prostitution as a child. She meets Michael Hosea, and God tells him he is to marry Angel and rescue her from the brothel. When I finished reading the book I said, "Lord, if you were to bring a man into my life just like Michael, I might consider marriage again some day." In the quiet moments that followed, my lonely heart began pounding, and my tears began to flow. The Holy Spirit spoke to my heart and said, "Phyllis, I am that Man."

I grieved my man so deeply. It felt like my heart hurt to even breathe. A friend invited me to go to a healing service at her church. It was in January, two and half years into my grief process. When the speaker asked anyone who needed healing to please stand, I, without even thinking, jumped to my feet. I started praying, asking God, "What do I need healing of?" The answer I heard was, "I am lifting this heavy grief off of you." I realized I was turning my wedding rings around and around. The voice said, "If you will take your wedding rings off, I will put a new ring on your finger. It will always remind you of Ron, your earthly husband. It will also remind you that now I am your Heavenly Husband. I am here to care for you and provide all your needs."

The Holy Spirit went on to tell me what the ring would look like. It would be two circles interlocked together. There would be three diamonds in the middle of the circles. The middle diamond would be larger than the two side diamonds. It was to remind me that God the Father, God the Son, and God the Holy Spirit would forever be with me. I drew a picture of what I had seen in my mind and took it to my jeweler. He looked through his books and said that it could not be done. He had oval sets that interlocked but not circles. I asked him to keep looking; I was going to Florida for a few weeks.

The last day in Florida, I stopped at this jewelry store to have a small diamond replaced that I had lost in a ring. While I was waiting I was looking in this case of different pieces of jewelry. There was my ring. I called to the jeweler in the back room. When he came out I asked, "May I see that ring?" My hands were shaking. I took off my wedding rings and slipped the beautiful new ring on my finger. It was a perfect fit. I began to tell him my story. I asked him where he had gotten this ring. He told me a lady had come into his shop and that she had designed it herself. She wanted him to find a jeweler to make it for her. He found a jeweler from Miami, Florida that was able to make it. His shop was in Bartov, a very small town. After the ring was made he contacted the lady, and she said because of health issues, she could not afford the ring. That was two days ago, so he put it in the case.

When I got back to Kentucky I called the jeweler and asked if he would call the lady and give her my phone number. I wanted to hear her story and why she had designed this ring. I never heard from her. I went to my jeweler in Kentucky to show him my ring. He was absolutely amazed when I showed him the ring. Whenever anyone asks me about my ring I tell them my story: how God, after Ron died, put a ring on my finger and made me His bride. The circles remind me that there is no beginning and no ending. When we receive Jesus as our Lord and Savior we will live with Him forever in eternity.

CHAPTER 27

MY SECOND MISSION TRIP TO THE PHILIPPINES

In 2008, I made my second trip to the Philippines. Pastor Billy promised this trip would not be as taxing because we would live on this fifty-two foot pontoon boat. Ron had been with Jesus for six years, so I felt the Holy Spirit encourage me to make the trip. I was sixty-eight years old then and beginning to have little health issues. We were far north near the China Sea on the east side of the large island of Luzon. There were no roads to get to the village, only paths or by boat.

The village was small, but there were other people that lived in the mountains that came down to fish in the ocean. We anchored there for two weeks, going from one little village to another in our small motorboat. When we went into the jungle village, Billy had me ride in a wooden sled. It was pulled by a water buffalo that I named Hazel. This area had many poisonous snakes—one bite and you would be with Jesus. We had three kinds of snakes we had to keep an open eye for—the sea snakes in the ocean as we walked to shore, the green snake, and the cobra that lived in the jungle.

These villages were not used to seeing white people or a clown, so we gathered big crowds for our programs. There are over three thousand islands in the Philippines. When the missionaries graduate from Bible school, they are to pray and ask God which island they are to take the Word of God to. They would then go to that island and make friends, teaching them the Bible. After they felt the time was right, Pastor Billy would bring a group of students and missionaries to that island and put on a crusade.

My bed on the boat was the size of an MRI tube. It was the grace of God I did not lose my mind on that trip. I would climb in feet first so my head would hang out of the opening. It was hot, hot, hot, and the boat rocked back and forth. This motion, believe me, did not put me to sleep. I would wet a washcloth and put it on my forehead. Then I would take my battery fan, prop it up to hit my washcloth, and then I would pray. Oh, how I prayed.

Many people in this village that lived on the sea received Jesus. They now wanted to build a small church where the other small villages could come and worship with them. One village man came asking if we wanted to buy his oceanfront land to build a church on it. I was so excited about this. Pastor Billy said there was no money to buy the land. My friends had donated money to help with my expenses. I knew this money was in Cebu, and I was going to use it to stay in this awesome resort before I returned to the States. I told Pastor Billy I had the money and, if I could stay in his home in Cebu, then we could buy the land. I walked along the oceanfront land, praying over it. I kept thanking God for using me to bless these people. I told the villagers I would build a church for them on the land. I talked to the Lord in prayer, and I said, "You know I am a giver, not a beggar." The Spirit spoke to my heart, giving me three people that would give five thousand dollars each to build the church.

We received word that there was a huge typhoon forming on the east side of the island where we were. It was decided that we would try to outrun it. We pulled up anchor and started back to the island of Cebu. We ran into waves that were fifteen to seventeen feet high, and our boat was overloaded with equipment and people. We were all very seasick and very frightened. You could hear people praying all over the boat.

After two days out in the storm, we lost the right rudder. Pastor Billy had taken his training in Florida and was a super pilot. He was able to hold the boat on the left side and ride the waves as if he was surfing. I was so sick that death was looking good to me. The Lord interrupted my thoughts and said, "Phyllis, you will not die. You have a church to build." When I told everyone what I had heard from God, a great peace came over our small boat. We made contact with a pastor as we got closer to Manila. We limped to shore, and they found someone to fix the rudder. Billy would not let me stay on the boat the remaining days. He had this pastor take me to Manila, and I flew back to Cebu. I waited in Cebu for Billy and the rest of the missionaries to return. When we saw the boat appear in the distance, we were crazy with joy. A ferry boat coming from Manila to Cebu went down during this storm, and hundreds were killed. Billy had told the pastor to fly me to Cebu and that I was not to take the ferry.

When I got back to the States, I called Shirley, Bill, and Dene. I told them about the need for a church in Palawan. They listened to my tearful story and said, "Yes, we will help build a church in Palawan." There is a beautiful church there today that we built and is also used for community meetings. I have a rooster made from seashells that is in my kitchen, reminding me how faithful God is. The rooster was presented to me by the village of Palawan honoring me as their friend.

"Heavens Doorway"—"Sonshine the Clown"
Filipino people

CHAPTER 28

OUR PRAYER THROUGH LOUISVILLE

On September 12, we met for an Aglow planning meeting for the International Aglow Conference of 2009 held in Louisville, Kentucky. Our prayer time was filled with God's presence as his Spirit touched different people and spoke words of encouragement to all. The Glory of God came down and filled that upper room. We were told that a word had come forth, that things would be happening in sets of four. The Spirit spoke to my heart and said, "I want you to drive around the downtown area of Louisville four times and do not walk. I am going to tear down the spiritual walls around the city."

As we exited from Highway 65 and turned onto First Street, the Spirit began to speak to our hearts. Whatever He said, we would pray it out. The Spirit said, "You are laying a grid today, and everyone within this grid will make Jesus Christ first in his or her life." Then we crossed Liberty Street. The Spirit said, "I will set the captives free and give them liberty." We drove to Broadway and again the Spirit spoke, "The people of Louisville have been on the broad way that leads to death, but I am going to reveal to them the straight and narrow way that will lead to eternal life." We were praising God for we knew that this was indeed a divine appointment.

We turned on Fourth, and there was a sign that read "Fourth Street Alive." Boldly, the Spirit spoke that all the partying people would grow dull with partying and would not be content until Jesus became their source of joy. We continued up Fourth Street, passing the convention center. There, we spoke blessings over the convention center and asked that God would station His guard angels at each door. If there were any attitudes that were disruptive and negative, they would be disarmed.

We drove under the Gault House, praying for all the leaders and committee worker's that would be staying there. We prayed that God would keep them healthy, provide protection, and empower them to do their jobs. As we turned onto River Road, the Spirit said that all of the words that the speakers spoke would become rivers of living water to all that heard them. By this time, we were shouting for joy. We then saw a sign that read, "High Voltage Overhead." We knew God was saying, "I am the powerful Almighty One. I will pour out my blessings over Louisville." When we turned right onto First Street, our second round of four, we saw a white horse pulling a white pumpkin coach with a driver and a little dog. Once more, the Spirit spoke that we were all Cinderella's, but He came and lifted us up from the miry pit and made us His bride. He has clothed us with white robes of righteousness. What an awesome first go-around; we now expected God to reveal much more as we drove on.

On the second, third, and fourth rounds, we prayed for people and businesses as we passed by. While driving down Fourth Street, Rose had a vision. These are Rose's words: "As Phyllis and I were doing a prayer drive around Louisville, God gave me a vision. On the second go-around, it was as if I was looking down on our route from above. I saw a large tube, and the tube was clear. You could see the buildings, the people, the cars, everything on the inside of the tube and on the outside. The tube was large. I would say, the size of three tires, side-by-side in diameter. It was filled with water, which burst, and the water gushed out onto everything surrounding the tube. Within the grid and outside the grid, it flowed. I felt that the Lord was saying that He was saturating the area with His Glory and pouring out Living Water that all may be free to partake.

On our third go-around, we continued to pray for people and businesses. On First Street, we again passed a Surgeon's Building at 444 First Street. Our prayer was that God would do surgery on the hearts of the people here in Louisville. Then on Fourth Street, near the convention center, we saw a lady we felt we were to pray with. When we asked her if there was anything that we could pray about with her, she was amazed. As she was walking, she was praying that God would reveal His will for her daughter. Her daughter was asked to go on a mission trip. We prayed for her and her daughter and felt led by the Spirit to give a gift for her daughter's mission trip. She thanked us, and we drove off. We were, by this time, rejoicing and praising

God for His love to us and for that lady. I later received a thank you card from the lady's daughter. She wanted me to know that she went on the mission trip, and it was a life-changing experience for her.

On our fourth go-around, we pulled to the side of the curb and asked God to be specific and show us who we should pray for. I saw a peace sign, and Rose saw a bow tie, so on this round, we were looking for a man. We drove up Fourth Street, they had blocked off a section of the street for the party crowd. We made a left turn, and when we did, the Spirit spoke that there will be many detours in life when we follow God, and we must be willing to take them. We were still looking for the man with the bow tie and the peace sign as we were getting close to completing our drive. In front of this wonderful Italian restaurant, sitting on a chair was a valet in a black suit, white shirt, and you guessed it, a bow tie. I went crazy in the Spirit, praising God. We pulled up to the curb and told him who we were. He said he was Persian and that his name meant integrity. Then we asked him if he would like a prayer for anything? He said yes. "Thursday, I will be taking an important test to be accepted into dental school." He then asked when we were going to pray. We said, "right now." The Spirit was powerful in praying for him. We told him that God had a plan for his life, and it was one for good, not evil. We said goodbye and that we would continue to pray for him. He thanked us and said, "God bless you." With that blessing, we left the city with our hearts overflowing with God's love.

I shared our prayer drive around Louisville with my small group from church. I made the comment that I was still looking for my peace sign. During our prayer time, the Lord spoke that He is the sign of peace that I saw in that powerful moment. He is the "Prince of Peace." The Spirit said that the soon coming worldwide Aglow Conference is covered with His peace. Louisville, Kentucky, is prepared for His will to be done due to the saints' obedience. The prophetic word was that the Heavenly realms are in place, holding back the forces of darkness and demonic forces to prevent confusion, turmoil, and every evil work. That there is one name that will make every demon flee, Jesus! "Praise and Glory and Honor be to the King of Kings and Lord of Lords." (Shalom)

On Friday, September 18, at my water aerobics class, I found my peace sign. One of the ladies had a small band-aid, the size of a dime on her arm. It was so small, if she had not been right next to me, I would not have been able to see it with my limited eyesight. There it was, a band-aid, shaped like a peace sign. I was so excited in my spirit. I asked the Lord if He would make a time that I could speak to her and pray for her. When we went to the wall to exercise, Carolyn ended up next to me. I told her about my experience and that I had been looking for a peace sign. She was moved to tears. I asked her if there was anything I could pray about for her. She shared some things with me and said what she needed in her life was peace. After we prayed, she told me that, under the peace sign band-aid, they had biopsied her arm for cancer. I told her that God loves her and was concerned about her life. So concerned that He spoke to me through His spirit, telling me to pray for a person with a peace sign. She was very touched because the roll of band-aids she had used was a roll with multiple designs and any design could have been on the top. God is awesome! Were those God's angels that led us and guided us through the city of Louisville, Kentucky? I believe they were angels then and still are guiding us today. That was many years ago, and the vale of the supernatural has become more transparent to me the older I become.

Rose and Phyllis
Women's Aglow 2009

CHAPTER 29

SEPTEMBER 26, 2009

Today, during our prayer time, Diane said that, "God was launching each one of us into ministry." I felt the Spirit say, "Look around you, look at your cities, look at your neighborhoods, do you not see? You do not need to go to the nations! I have brought the nations to you!" I felt I was in a liquid substance, and I needed to surface immediately or I would drown. I seemed to be in the middle of a bubble. I knew I did not have enough time to go down and reach the bottom to push myself up to break the surface of the bubble. I cried out to the Lord to help me. My arms straightened over my head, in a diving position, and instantly, I was a rocket being shot to the surface. When I broke the liquid bubble and surfaced, I was gasping for air. I was very aware of the beautiful sky and a larger world around me. Everything looked the same, but it was so much larger than the small world I had just left. I looked down, and I began to see all these lights as if small rockets were being launched. It looked like a firework display that I was watching from an airplane. I asked God what was happening? He spoke to me and said, "These are all the people that I am launching into world missions. I have seated you and surrounded you in my bubble of love since your birth, providing for your every need. You have been growing in my womb and now is the time for you to be born for what I created you to be. The world, as you know it, is no longer your neighborhood, your family, your friends, and your church. I am going to use you to be my hands, my heart, and my presence in the larger hurting world around you. Do not be afraid, for you and I are one, seated in the Heavenlies."

CHAPTER 30

I HAD A DREAM OR PERHAPS A VISION—I DO NOT KNOW

Sunday, February 1, 2014, ICU at Norton Hospital in Louisville, Kentucky. I was praying and singing at bedtime, "I will enter His gates with thanksgiving in my heart, I will enter His courts with praise, I will say this is the day that the Lord has made, I will rejoice for He has made me glad."

I saw a large rock with a shaft of light coming out of the Heavens. I fell upon the rock and knew I had fallen upon *Jesus*, for He is my rock and my salvation. As I was worshiping, I looked up and saw angels ascending and descending. I heard a voice say, "Come!"

As I started climbing the ladder of angels, I would take the angel down and stack it in a pile in my left hand. I kept going up the ladder but had the feeling of standing in one place. I rejoiced with each angel I gathered, and then another angel would appear and replace the one I had taken down.

It seemed like a long time of being surrounded by angels. Then I appeared on the top of the ladder. I stood looking into the Heavens. It was absolutely beautiful, simply awesome. Each of the objects there was very colorful. Then I saw a person walking toward me, and I knew it was King Jesus. I could not see His face because of the bright light. He was dressed in a golden white robe. As He came near, He covered me with His robe as I knelt before Him in worship. This is the third time since I became ill that He has appeared to me in like manner.

Then I was aware of being back in bed, and Jesus spoke again. "Every angel you have gathered is to be given to a person of my choice to be their personal ministering angel. This angel has been chosen for you as a reminder God loves you and you're never alone."

"Are not all angels ministering spirits sent to save those who will inherit salvation?" (Hebrew 1:14)

Blessings!

Always with you
Never Judge you
Give you guidance every day
Enfold you in their healing wings
Love you unconditional
Support you in every way

ANGELS
Everyone has an ANGEL
Given to us from the START,
Trust and FAITH is what we
need to hear them in our HEART.

Authors unknown

CHAPTER 31

AN ANGEL SAID: MOVE TO MINNESOTA

I had been very sick between the years 2012 and 2014. I had a double knee surgery, then a right rotator cuff surgery, and finally brain surgery in the fall of 2013. The following year, 2014, I had been hospitalized three times because my hormonal system was always shutting down. On April 22, 2015, I woke up with a start in my bedroom. I felt there was someone in the room. My room got very bright, and I heard a voice say, "Move to Minnesota." I lay there the rest of the night, trying to process what this could possibly mean. I was so sick I knew I was unable to pack a suitcase, let alone move.

Two days later, my daughter, Julie, called and asked, "Mother, would you like to move to Minnesota?" I said, "Yes, but how can I even think of moving when I feel so ill?" She said, "There are people we can hire to pack your belongings and move you."

The rest is history. His Story. God has provided everything I could need and even more. I was born in Forest City, Iowa, so moving to Minnesota felt like I had come home. On the day

I put up the "For Sale" sign in the front yard of my Kentucky home, the door bell rang. There stood a tall, very pretty lady. She asked me, "Is your home for sale?" I said, "Yes, it is." With that, she responded, "My name is Joan. Do not sell it until you hear from me. I am a serious cash buyer from California. I will be here tomorrow with my realtor. Remember my name is Joan, so do not sell until you have heard from me." This was a God thing! I want you to hear Joan's testimony:

My Move to Louisville, Kentucky
by Joan

When my home was sold in California, I was in Louisville, Kentucky, visiting my son and looking for a condo to buy to live near him. After a week of looking, I needed to return to California. My son is a pilot for Delta Airlines, so when I fly, I fly standby. I left Louisville and flew to Atlanta, Georgia, to make my connecting flight, but there were no openings from there to Sacramento, California. My son said, "Come back to Louisville and we will try getting you out in a few days."

When I returned to Louisville, it was late afternoon. On the way back to his home, my son suggested that we drive through a nice residential area we both liked. As we were driving through that nice area with winding streets, suddenly, there it was, a "For Sale" sign! We stopped and were very excited! My son strongly advised me to go to the door and make a contact! I did and that's when the divine appointment happened! Phyllis came to the door, and I blurted out, "My name is Joan" and that I was a serious cash buyer from California. I said, "Please don't sell the house to anyone else!" Phyllis was not feeling well but was so polite and accommodating. We soon discovered we were both Christians and ended up praying for each other's needs. The next day, my realtor had made a morning appointment with Phyllis' agent to see the house. The minute I walked in and looked around, I knew this was to be my house. We made an offer at list price, and it was accepted!

Wow, how awesome God was to orchestrate all the fine details. My travel delay was just to keep me in the area until that "For Sale" sign went into the ground. There is more. Phyllis told my son that her home had been the weekly meeting place of her Life Group for her church. New Life Church is now my church, and I continue to host the Life Group meetings as Phyllis did. This has so pleased me and fulfilled God's plan for the house and my ministry. God is indeed awesome. His thoughts and ways are higher than ours!

My Grandchildren
Mitchell, Jaclyn, Nonne, Saffron, Merlyn

My Family
Brikken, Merlyn, Edison, Drew, Julie
Nonne, Jaclyn, Mitchell

CHAPTER 32

THANK YOU, LOUISVILLE

My move from my old Kentucky home in Louisville, Kentucky, to Minnesota was orchestrated by God. It will remain one of the hardest, most painful things God has ever asked me to do. It took me six weeks before I could share with my son, Ron, and his family that I was planning to move to Minnesota. It was a week later before I told my dear neighbors and friends. There were so many blessings for me while living in Louisville. I met many wonderful people and had great neighbors and a loving church family. Everything and everybody has been etched on my heart forever. There wasn't anything I did not like about Louisville. My husband, Ron, had died thirteen months after our move to Kentucky.

It really helped me to have my grandchildren there during my long grief journey. They would often spend the night with me. We would go to plays or movies and out to eat. Other times we would go to the dollar store and then back to the house to work on our crafts. Our last stop was always to pick up doughnuts for our breakfast the next day.

We would often go out to dinner at the Olive Garden. It was our favorite restaurant then and still is today. Jaclyn and Mitchell were a source of joy to me in my grief journey. They were young and liked to remember Popa and talk about him. It was so good for me to talk about him then and still is today. We created a game; we would play "I love you more!" After we settled in bed for the night, we would take turns saying, "How much! Do you love me more?"

Ronnie, you will always be my favorite son. Kristi, you will always be my favorite daughter-in-love. Jaclyn, Mitchell, Jared, and all my dear friends in Louisville, I love you more than all the ice cream in the world. Blessings!

Nonne

My Kentucky Derby Hat

The Kentucky Family
Back row: Kristi and Ron
Front row: Mitchell, Jared, Jaclyn

CHAPTER 33

SETTLING IN MINNESOTA

My move to Minnesota in 2015 has been a huge joy and a blessing. The neighborhood I moved into is friendly, and the houses are really cute. We have twenty-one single family homes. Each home has two bedrooms, two baths, and a sunroom. We also have these neat porches. My home faces the Mississippi River, so I can often watch the eagles soaring in the sky. There are four of us ladies who love to play Rummikub each week. We all enjoy the game and each other.

The church that I joined is only five minutes away. I'm in a small group of men and women of different ages from our church. We meet at one another's homes once a month for potluck and to study the Word. I am also in a group of godly ladies at church called Women of Glory that meet weekly for study and fellowship. They are a huge support and are so loving and kind to me.

Over the years, I would only see Julie and her family two or three times a year at most. To live this close to my (Jewel) Julie and her family is a fairy tale come true. Julie's family lives only twelve minutes from me. When Julie was born, I felt I had received a special girlfriend.

Julie spent weeks on line looking for a place for me to live. She and the family than spent weeks making my house into a home. Thank you Julie and Drew, Brikken,Merlyn, saffron,and Edison you were all a huge blessing to me. My son-in-love, Drew, is so tender and dear to me.

He is our driver. My husband, Ron, always referred to himself as the driver. It now feels so grand to have my own private driver once again. My firstborn granddaughter, Brikken, called me when she picked up her new car. She said, "Do you want to go for a ride, Nonne?" I'm sure I responded, "Absolutely!"

In 2016, she brought me her dirndl dress from Germany. She, Julie, and I went to the October German Fest. Drew was our driver. He dropped us off, and when we were ready to leave, he came back for us. What fun! When my granddaughter, Miss Merlyn, is in town from college, she spends the night with me. These are becoming precious memories for me. I now call my guest room Merlyn's Room. My granddaughter, Saffron, gave me a great gift of herself and time when I moved here. I lived with Julie and the family for seven weeks while looking for my own place. Saffron drove my car around the area to log driving time for her driver's license. It wasn't until I was on my own that I realized how much Saffron had taught me about the new area I was living in.

When our German exchange student, May, was coming to live with us, I needed to give up my bedroom. I was living with Julie and her family at the time. Where to put

Nonne? Eddy, my twelve-year-old grandson, told me that I could share his room with him. My sweet Edison shared not only his room with me but also his tender heart of love with me. *I love you more!* Thanks, family, for making my move to Minnesota a loving experience.

Blessings!

Nonne

Nonne and Brikken in their dirndl dresses (2016)

My Minnesota Family
Back row: Edison, Saffron, Merlyn, Brikken
Front row: Drew, Julie

CHAPTER 34

ANGEL AT CUB FOOD STORE

I had moved to Minnesota in 2015 and was missing my friends from Kentucky. We are only a block from the Mississippi River where I love watching the eagles soar in the sky. I moved into my home the end of August, and I had only met a few of my neighbors. Fall was fast giving way to winter. I had been told horror stories of snowstorms in Minnesota. I did not want to go through a hard winter without knowing my neighbors. I had a feeling I should go to each house and introduce myself, letting them know I was their new neighbor. Everyone welcomed me and was so sweet and kind. Minnesota was now feeling more like home to me. My health was not very good, but my spirit was filled with a new joy. I wanted to have an open house for my new friends and neighbors. I sent an invitation to all twenty-one homes, inviting them to my open house Christmas party. My daughter, Julie, said she would help me with whatever I needed. I began preparing to host the Christmas open house. I went shopping at the Cub Food Store for all the goodies that I would be serving. Even though it was Saturday, there were only three people in my line. There was a young lady in front of me. She had a child in her shopping cart, about five years old. Behind me was a lady who did not seem to have anything. She stood with her hands in her pockets. I asked her if she wanted to go in front of me. She shook her head and said, "No, thank you." The young woman in front of me had forgotten her government food card in her car. The cashier said he had to have her food card because he had already rung up the groceries. I told her, "Go to your car and get your card, I will watch your child." She ran out of the store, and soon she was back with her food card. I turned to the lady behind me and again asked, "Would you like to go ahead of me?" Again, she responded, "No, thank you." A lot of time had now gone by standing in this checkout line. There still was no one standing behind her. I once again, was aware of the fact that both of her hands were in her pockets. The cashier rang up my order, and it came to over eighty dollars. The lady behind me went into action. She moved around me with lightning speed. She took a Cub gift card and swiped it through the machine. I looked at her amazed and somewhat confused, asking her, "What are you doing?"

She answered, "Paying for your groceries."

I said, "Thank you," and wrapped my arms around her, giving her a hug. I then looked at the cashier and asked, still confused, "What did she do?"

He said, "She paid for your groceries." We both looked in the direction she had gone, and there was no sign of her. The young man said he had never seen anything like this happen before in his life. I asked him, "Do you think she was an angel?"

Was she an earthly angel or a Heavenly angel? My feeling is she was from Heaven because there was so much peace about her as she waited in line. Whoever she was, either an earth angel or Heavenly angel, they are to bring God's love to His people, and love is what I received that day.

CHAPTER 35

LOST GOLD EARRING 2017

In January of 2017, Drew, my son-in-love, had driven me to my eye doctor's appointment. It had been snowing, so the parking lot had a few inches of snow that had turned into slush. The eye doctor's office was filled with many people. I didn't notice, nor did anyone else, that I was missing an earring. After the appointment, Drew was going to help me into the passenger side of the car. He stopped me and said, "Phyllis, look." There on the passenger side on the handle of the car was my gold earring.

As the sun landed on the gold earring, it reflected back a light beam shining toward the sky. We were probably three to four feet away from the car door when Drew saw it. He went over to the car door and picked up my gold earring. Then he turned to me and said, "Phyllis, is this your earring?" I was so stunned. I wasn't even aware that I had only one earring on. We marveled at how that earring could lie on the door handle. What kept it from falling into the slushy snow in the parking lot? Who found it and laid my earring on the door handle? What kept it from being blown off the car door handle by the wind and into the snow? There are angels all around us—some are earth angels, others angelical angels. I, for one, am so very thankful for all the help God sends my way through his ministering angels.

CHAPTER 36

THE ANGELS THAT HELD MY HANDS 2018

Five years ago, in Kentucky, I had an epidural in my back. They thought the pain in my knees was coming from my back and spine. The doctor used a contrast dye in the shot that I was extremely allergic to. I was in bed four days with muscle spasms and could not walk for two days. My chronic pain has increased since I moved to Minnesota. My spine doctor here wanted to try it once again. When I explained what happened to me in Kentucky, he was also hesitant. After receiving my records, he knew why. I had a severe reaction to the shots because of the contrast dye they had used. I finally agreed to move forward and have the shots once again. When I arrived at my appointment, my prayer was for my doctor and his assistants. Then I asked Father God to release His angels to encourage me and keep me in His perfect peace. They had me lay on my tummy on the table.

The assistants arranged the pillow around my chest, making me more comfortable. It was then that I had a vision experience with four angels. They all seemed so excited and happy that they were the ones chosen to serve me. My hands were open in front of my pillow. I then felt and heard this sweet voice say, "I will take her right hand." Then I felt someone else take my left hand. I could feel the presence of movement all around me. I had the sense that the other two angels were at my right and left side standing by the doctor.

I heard a voice say, "Now squeeze our hands, and we will receive your pain from you." Then the doctor began to talk me through the procedure. He was on my right side and said, "You will now feel a prick and then a little pain." I instantly felt someone squeezing my hand as he worked on my right side but no pain. The doctor then moved to my left side and again told me what he was going to do. He said, "You will feel a prick and then a little pain." Once again, I felt someone squeeze my left hand but no pain. Later that night when I got home, I was reminded when my children were young and needed shots, I would always have them hold my hand and tell them to "squeeze it hard. I will take all your pain from you." My Daddy in Heaven was so concerned about His little girl He sent His angels to meet my every need. My heart is so filled with great joy that our Father God cares so much about each one of us. Ask God to open your spiritual eyes to see how His Heavenly angels are always providing and protecting you. We indeed have angels all around us.

CHAPTER 37

MY SEVENTY-EIGHTH
BIRTHDAY 2018

How awesome is our God. Angels bow before Him, and we can do no less. God in His great love wanted me to know this. God was with me at my birth and He will be with me in my old age. "Even to your old age and gray hairs I am He, I am He who will sustain you. I made you and I will carry you; I will sustain you and I will rescue you." (Isaiah 46:4) "Gray hair is a crown of splendor; it is attained in the way of righteousness." (Proverbs 16:31)

On Saturday night, December 1, 2018, I was looking for my file of Christmas labels. I found an envelope with two homemade anniversary cards in it. Ron and I had made these cards for one another on our thirty-ninth wedding anniversary in 1999. We were at Julie's house in Minnesota for a computer camp she had designed for us. Julie remembers helping Ron and me make these cards. It was a great joy to read them. To see those words of encouragement and of our love to one another.

At church the next morning our pastor said, that "because of a retreat I was attending I had prepared my sermon on Friday. The Holy Spirit spoke to me at the end of the retreat on Saturday saying to "put the sermon on the Altar." God had something else He wanted him to share with the church. He asked us to get into groups of two and three and share a memory, either a recent memory or one from the past. I shared about finding these anniversary cards the night before that were nineteen years old. Ron had already begun to have health issues in 1999. I do not remember making these cards or ever seeing them before. Pastor's message was "Rise and Shine and Let Your Light Shine." That is hard to do when there are areas of our lives, he said, where we still need healing. He ended his message by asking us to go back to the memory we had shared at the beginning of the service. Pastor Carl said, ''Now bring Jesus into that memory." What was needed or still is needed in your memory? Was it forgiveness, healing, acceptance, or love? He asked us to pray and meditate on the memory and bring Jesus into it. The church became very quiet as people were praying and remembering. You could feel the presence of God and His angels at work in the hearts of His people. In that holy moment I had a vision of my Ron in Heaven. He was so happy surrounded with his Heavenly family and friends. In this vision, someone announced that I was there, and everyone rushed over to me and began giving me hugs. I can still feel those hugs today. Pastor began to speak again, and my brief vision was over. On Monday, December the 3rd, my 78th birthday, I started writing my story. God reminded me that I had asked Him on October the 5th to wish my man a happy 80th birthday in Heaven. Later in the day I heard the Lord speak so softly saying, "Phyllis, Ron is very happy sharing his birthday with his Heavenly family. He has his daughter Sherri Lynn, and grandson, Jared, with him. He is laughing with his parents and yours. Your Aunt Olive and your friends, Sue and Pat, are also there." I began to laugh and then cry as I thanked God that he would speak those thoughts into my mind. Our Sherri Lynn left her earthly body on December 13, 1970 to be with Jesus. I have always celebrated December 13 alone but not anymore. On June 2, 2019 we had memorial bricks laid in honor of Sherri Lynn, our daughter, and Jared, our grandson, in Maple Grove, Minnesota, in "The Angel of Hope Gardens" which exist throughout our country. On December 6th the foundation holds a candle lighting ceremony honoring all children that have passed. This idea for "Angel of Hope" came from a book written 20 years ago called, "The Christmas Box" by Richard Paul Evans. I rejoice with each one of you that has a loved one that now makes their home in Heaven. We need to keep their memories alive. We all have our stories to tell. Tell your stories. We are all blessed and highly favored of the Lord.

"Let all you do today be done in love." (1 Corinthians 16:14)

In Kentucky at the Glitz on my 70th Birthday
Charlene, Claire, Phyllis, Joan, Minnie

78th Birthday with my family in Minnesota.
Edison, Julie, Merlyn, Brikken, Phyllis, Saffron, Drew

Dedication of bricks for
Sherri Lynn and Jared
June 2, 2020
Mitchell, Kristi, Ron, Phyllis

" Let all you do today
be done in LOVE"
1 Corinthian 16:16

Painting by Evette

Four things God wants you to know.

1. You need to be saved from sin's penalty.
   For all have sinned, and fall short of the glory of God (Romans 6:23)

2. You cannot save yourself.
   Jesus said to him, I am the way, and the truth, and the life. No one comes to the Father except through me". (John 14:)

3. Jesus has provided for your salvation.
   God so loved the world that he gave his only son, that whoever believes in him should not perish but have eternal life. (John 3:16)

4. You can have eternal life today.
   Whoever hears my word and belives has passed from death to life, (John 5:24)

THE RED HEART

As you touch this little red heart, let it be a reminder to you, that God has shed His blood on the cross for you and me. There are not any magical powers in this heart, it is just a point of contact. "Amazing love how can it be that you our Lord would die for me." But You did die for us out of Your great love for each one of us. God loves each one of us unconditionally. His great love for us is why He chose to die for our sins, so that we can live with Him forever. When we die we are "absent from our body and present with my Lord." I love each one of you and want to see you and be with you in Heaven. This can only be possible if you are a believer in Jesus Christ. "Sonshine the Clown" has given this altar call in many countries and states. The salvation message is a very simple one;

(1) You must A – ACCEPT and receive Jesus Christ as your Lord and Savior.
(2) You then B – BELIEVE that you were born in sin and that the blood shed at the cross will take away your sin. Believe that God will forgive ALL your sins.
(3) Now C – you CONFESS to others giving a witness to the miracle of His perfecting love in your

hearts'. Trust me if you do ABC you will experience a new life filled with peace and joy with many blessings.

Thank you for listening to my heart and the heart of Jesus. Oh, how I love each one of you, my family and friends. It is my heart's desire that I spend all eternity with you in Heaven. I am unable to take anything with me to Heaven but you.
I love you more! Sonshine the Clown
Let this not be a *goodbye* but an "I will see you soon!"

Assuredly, I say to you, unless you are converted and become as little children, you will by no means enter the kingdom of heaven. Therefore whoever humbles himself as this little child is the greatest in the kingdom of heaven. (Matthew 18:3-4)

Scarlet my little Earth Angel holding Angel Doll

My great grandparents church
in unterampfrach Germany

THE REVELATIONS OF
SCRIPTURE ON ANGELS

(*Unger's Bible Dictionary*, pp 52.):

- They furnish a necessary safeguard against narrowness of thought as to the extent and variety of the creations of God.
- They help us in acquiring the proper conception of Christ, who is above the angels and the object of angelic worship.
- They give a wonderful attractiveness to our conception of that unseen world to which we are hastening.
- They set before us an example of joyous and perfect fulfillment of God's will. "Thy will be done on earth as it is in Heaven," by angels.
- They put to shame the horrible indifference of multitudes of mankind with respect to the great work of conversion. There is joy among the angels over one sinner that repented.
- They broaden our view of manifold mercies of God, whose angels are "sent forth to minister for them who shall be heirs of salvation" (Hebrews 1:14).

- They remind us of our high rank as human beings and our exalted destiny as Christians. We, who are "made but little lower than the angels," may become as the angels of God in Heaven (Psalm 8:5) "lower than God" (Matthew 22:30).
- Angels will be the harvesters in the end (Matthew 13:39).
- Angels will execute judgment in the end (Matthew 13:24, 50).
- We have our own guardian angels (Matthew 18:10).
- We will be as angels in Heaven (Matthew 22:30).
- When Jesus comes again, all the angels will come with him (Matthew 25:31).
- Jesus could have called ten thousand angels to save his life (Matthew 26:15).
- The angels will rejoice when one sinner comes home (Luke 15:10).
- When we die, angels will carry us to Heaven (Luke 16:22).
- God commands the angels to guard and protect us (Psalm 91:11).
- We are only a little lower than the angels (Psalm 8:5).
- Angels are sent to minister to them who shall be heirs of salvation (Hebrews 1:14).
- Christ is greater than angels (Hebrews 15:14).
- The angels are serving in Heaven (Revelation 8:9).
- The angels are spiritual warriors fighting when called upon (Revelation 12:7–12).
- The angels sang the song "Worthy Is the Lamb" in Heaven (Revelation 5:11–12).

ACKNOWLEDGMENTS

I am so thankful and blessed by all my sisters and brothers in Christ. To my precious friend Nanette, you spoke into the airwaves, saying, "Phyllis, you really need to put your stories on paper for your family to read." The Lord began to encourage me that we all have our stories that need to be told.

To Jean, who blesses me with her poems and songs often when I'm needing encouragement, I knew for this to become a book, it would be another one of those miracles in my life. All honor and glory to God who has provided me with all that I need.

To Pastor Dick, Barb, Mary Ann, Cheryl, Lee, and Wendy who have been a huge blessing to me, thank you all for being so willing to give of your time to read and edit my stories. You have given me hope and encouragement. When I was working on the manuscript after my major eye surgery, I was reminded again that these stories are written down to bless my family and friends and remind all of us how much God cares for each one of us.

For my book cover, I wanted an angel that would inspire peace, love, and joy—one that would make you feel protected, secure, and safe in its presence. I am blessed and feel so connected with Mary Lou's paintings, and I am very thankful she said yes to me.

I am forever grateful to all of you. Thank you! We are blessed and highly favored.

Honored Ron and my 60th wedding
anniversary on September 3rd 2020

GAP Girls
God Answerers Prayer
Back row—Kay, Phyllis, Marilyn, Ann, Gin, Dene, Phyllis
Front row—Judy, Sharon, Sharon, Sylvia, Libby

ANGELS bring you Strength...

ANGELS AROUND US (2018)

Angels, angels everywhere
Visualized or not—do we care?
God sends them down to us
They are helpers we can trust
There's no place where angels fear to tread
Not humans—but spiritual beings instead
Messengers, a safety net, a helping hand
Let us realize they're in our land
Behind the scenes—the unseen ones
God's ministering spirits in a world that is fallen
Ask for them to be sent—ask God to call them
Jeremiah 33:3—God's telephone number
Call Him—ask for release of angels from His Heaven
God's messengers, protection, help in time of need
God's angels are working daily
Believe—Receive—Indeed

Jean

"Call to me and I will answer you and tell you great and mighty things you do not know" (Jeremiah 33:3).

Women of Glory
Back row—Barbara, Linda, Becky, Nanette, Kay, Sheila, Jean, Barbara
Front row—Beverly, Sylvia, Phyllis, Nancy

Ron and Phyllis in the late 70's

ABOUT THE AUTHOR

Ron in his Air Force
uniform (1957)

Ron and I sitting on the
moon (1959)
at Riverside Amusement
Park in Chicago

Phyllis (Miss Nonne), lives in Minnesota and has three children as well as seven grandchildren. She is originally from Iowa
and lived in Chicago for ten years and Libertyville, Illinois, for
thirty-two years. She and her husband Ron enjoyed traveling
and have visited each state in the country. They also had the
privilege to travel to different parts of the world. In 2002 they
moved to Louisville, Kentucky to be near their son and family.
Miss Nonne's sweet husband passed away in 2003. She lived
in Kentucky until God called her to Minnesota to be close to
her daughter, Julie, and her family. She has been blessed and
encouraged by God's people in every state she lived in.

"The angel of the Lord encamps around those
Who fear Him, and He delivers them."
Psalm 34:7

CPSIA information can be obtained
at www.ICGtesting.com
Printed in the USA
LVHW070324141021
700408LV00017B/806

9 781645 591979